TAILGATING
ESSENTIALS COOKBOOK

Recipe selection, design, and book design © 2022 by Anne Schaeffer and
Fox Chapel Publishing Company, Inc., 903 Square Street, Mount Joy, PA 17552.
Recipes and photography © 2019 Rada Mfg DBA CQ Products.

ISBN 978-1-4971-0301-6

Library of Congress Control Number: 2021953489

Shutterstock credits: Africa Studio (pages 4–5); Anucha Tiemsom (pages 2–3
background); Binh Thanh Bui (page 72 bottom left); Gita Kulinitch Studio (page 72
bottom right); majson (football icon throughout, helmet icon on page 78); Mtsaride
(page 1); Sean Locke Photography (pages 3, 6–7); Serenethos (page 171)

To learn more about the other great books from Fox Chapel Publishing,
or to find a retailer near you, call toll-free
800-457-9112 or visit us at *www.FoxChapelPublishing.com*.

We are always looking for talented authors. To submit an idea, please send a brief
inquiry to acquisitions@foxchapelpublishing.com.

Printed in China
First printing

TAILGATING
ESSENTIALS **COOKBOOK**

150 WINNING GAME-DAY RECIPES FOR
BEVERAGES, SNACKS, MAIN DISHES, AND MORE

ANNE SCHAEFFER

FOX CHAPEL
PUBLISHING

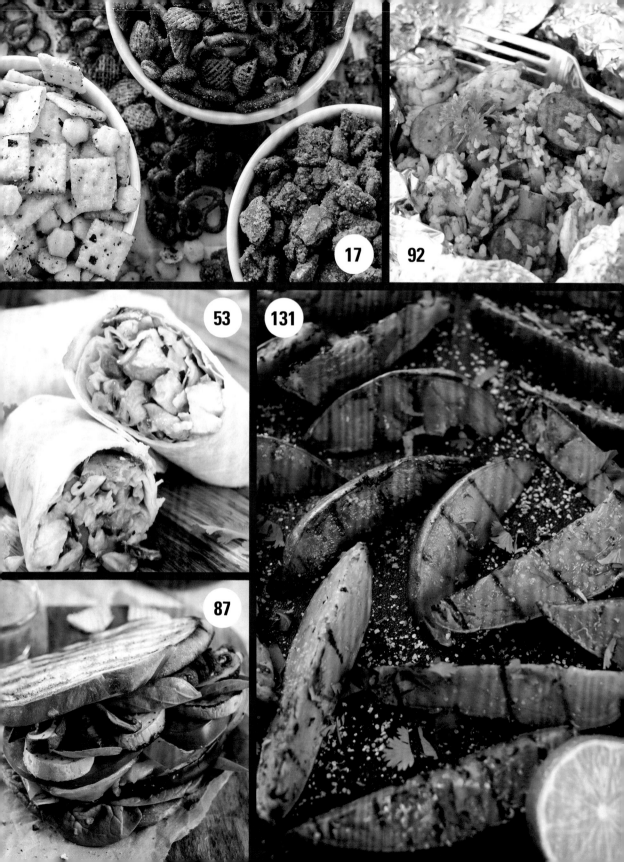

17

92

53

131

87

119

141

166

CONTENTS

FRIENDS, FOOD & FANDOM

In this book, I'm giving you the yummiest recipes to help you pull off an awesome tailgating menu. To get started, here are a few of my favorite tips for pre-game success.

- ✗ Prepare as much of the food as possible in advance. Premix your drinks, marinate your chicken, make the dips, and pack the cookies.

- ✗ If you're headed to the game, check the venue's website for tailgating rules so there are no surprises when you arrive.

- ✗ Frozen bottles of water will not only keep food cold in your cooler, it will also give you ice-cold drinking water as the ice melts.

- ✗ Make sure you have more fuel or charcoal for your grill than you think you'll need. Also, think about how you'll pack and bring home a dirty grill.

- ✗ Heavy-duty aluminum foil and disposable foil pans are great for reheating food on the grill.

- ✗ Car power socket-compatible slow cookers are great for keeping chilis and dips warm, but I still recommend actually making them ahead of time.

- ✗ Take trash bags or big plastic bins for hauling out your trash when you leave.

- ✗ Pack a few portable chairs and a folding table.

- ✗ Using a tablecloth makes for easier cleanup, no matter where you are.

- ✗ Disposable wet wipes or good ol' soap and water are a must for messy fingers. I do not recommend wiping hands on game day jerseys!

APPS & SNACKS

CHOCOLATE CHIP MUFFINS

🏈 MAKES 6 🏈

- ✗ 4 T. unsalted butter
- ✗ ¼ C. vegetable oil
- ✗ Sugar
- ✗ 1 egg
- ✗ 1 egg white
- ✗ 1½ tsp. vanilla
- ✗ ½ C. buttermilk
- ✗ 1¾ C. flour
- ✗ 2 tsp. baking powder
- ✗ 2 tsp. cornstarch
- ✗ ½ tsp. salt
- ✗ 1 C. semi-sweet chocolate chips

In a glass mixing bowl, melt the butter in the microwave; cool 5 minutes, then stir in the oil. Add 1 cup of sugar, the egg, egg white, and vanilla and stir until well combined. Stir in the buttermilk.

In a separate bowl, mix the flour, baking powder, cornstarch, and salt. Fold the dry ingredients into the wet ingredients until barely combined and then gently stir in the chocolate chips until just combined (*don't overmix*). Cover the bowl with a towel and let rest 15 minutes. Meanwhile, preheat the oven to 425°F.

Line jumbo muffin tins with liners and divide the batter among them. Sprinkle the top of each muffin with about 1 tablespoon sugar and bake for 8 minutes; keep muffins in the oven while you reduce the heat to 350°F and bake 15 minutes longer, until tops are just beginning to turn golden.

RASPBERRY LEMON COFFEE CAKE

🏈 SERVES 12 🏈

- ✗ 1¾ C. sugar, divided
- ✗ 2⅔ C. flour, divided
- ✗ ¾ C. butter (½ C. cold, ¼ C. softened), divided
- ✗ ¾ C. milk
- ✗ 1 (5.3 oz.) container plain Greek yogurt
- ✗ 1 egg
- ✗ 1 T. finely grated lemon zest
- ✗ 3 to 4 T. lemon juice, divided
- ✗ 2½ tsp. baking powder
- ✗ 1½ C. fresh raspberries, plus more for serving
- ✗ ½ C. powdered sugar

Preheat the oven to 350°F and grease a 9 x 13" baking pan. Combine 1 cup sugar and ⅔ cup flour; slice the cold butter and cut into the dry ingredients until crumbly; set aside.

In a mixing bowl, beat together the milk, yogurt, egg, lemon zest, 2 tablespoons lemon juice, the remaining ¾ cup sugar, and the softened butter until creamy. In a small bowl, stir together the baking powder and the remaining 2 cups of the flour and beat into the creamy mixture until just blended. Fold in 1½ cups raspberries. Spread the batter into the prepped pan and sprinkle evenly with the set-aside crumb topping. Bake 45 to 50 minutes or until a toothpick inserted comes out with a few crumbs. Set aside until cool.

Mix the powdered sugar with the remaining 1 to 2 tablespoons lemon juice and drizzle over the cooled coffee cake. Serve with more raspberries.

PEANUT & CRACKER JACK BARS

🏈 **MAKES 12** 🏈

Preheat the oven to 350°F and butter a 9 x 13" baking pan; line with parchment paper, letting about 1" hang over two sides. Set aside.

In a mixing bowl, beat together 1 cup melted butter and 1¼ cups brown sugar until smooth. Add 2 eggs, one at a time, beating well after each. Mix in 1 teaspoon vanilla and ½ teaspoon salt; add 2 cups flour and beat until just incorporated. Gently fold in ½ cup chopped salted peanuts and spread batter evenly in the prepped pan; sprinkle with 3 heaping cups Cracker Jacks and ¼ cup chopped salted peanuts, pressing down gently to adhere.

Bake 25 to 30 minutes, until golden brown and firm to the touch. Set aside to cool. Remove from the pan using the parchment paper and cut into squares.

CLASSIC DEVILED EGGS

- ✗ 6 eggs
- ✗ 2 T. mayo
- ✗ 1½ T. sweet pickle relish
- ✗ 1 tsp. prepared yellow mustard
- ✗ ⅛ tsp. salt
- ✗ Dash of black pepper
- ✗ Paprika

Put the eggs in a single layer in a saucepan and add water to cover by 1". Bring to a boil; cover, remove from the heat, and let stand 15 minutes.

Drain the water off the eggs, then fill the saucepan with cold water and ice; let stand until the eggs are cool.

Peel the eggs under cold running water and slice them in half lengthwise. Using a spoon, remove the yolks and toss them into a bowl along with the mayo, relish, mustard, salt, and black pepper; mash and stir until well combined. Spoon the yolk mixture into hollowed-out egg whites and sprinkle with paprika.

HUDDLE UP!

Need a break from heavy tailgating food? Far from boring, this unique hummus is the perfect combination of sweet and smoky.

SMOKY HUMMUS

🏈 MAKES 1½ CUPS 🏈

Drain 1 (15 oz.) can chickpeas, reserving the liquid. Rinse the chickpeas under cold water and dump into a food processor. Add 2 roasted red bell peppers, ½ cup sun-dried tomato halves, ¼ cup tahini, 1 chopped garlic clove, and 3 tablespoons olive oil; pulse until relatively smooth.

With the machine running, slowly add 5 tablespoons of the reserved chickpea liquid; season with salt, black pepper, cayenne pepper, and paprika to taste. Portion out into individual serving bowls for easy eating. Serve with fresh veggies (*try carrots, tomatoes, bell peppers, cucumbers, and zucchini*).

TAILGATE TIP

Plan to arrive at least four hours before the game and eat at least two hours before the game. Then you'll have plenty of time to set up and clean up.

WALKING VEGGIES

Put some hummus in the bottom of small cups and fill with veggies for individual servings. Make as many as you need.

HUMMUS WITH VEGGIES

🏈 SERVINGS VARY 🏈

- ✗ ¼ C. tahini
- ✗ ¼ C. fresh lemon juice
- ✗ 2 T. olive oil, plus more for serving
- ✗ 1 garlic clove, minced
- ✗ ½ tsp. ground cumin
- ✗ Salt
- ✗ 1 (15 oz.) can chickpeas (garbanzo beans), drained & rinsed
- ✗ 2 to 3 T. water
- ✗ Paprika for serving
- ✗ Your favorite fresh veggies for dipping

In the bowl of a food processor, combine the tahini and lemon juice and process for 1½ minutes, scraping the sides and bottom of the bowl once. Add 2 tablespoons oil, the garlic, cumin, and ½ teaspoon salt and process for 1 minute, until well blended, scraping the bowl once. Add half the chickpeas and process for 1 minute; scrape the bowl. Add the remaining chickpeas and process for 1 to 2 minutes, until thick and quite smooth. With the food processor running, slowly add the water through the chute, until the hummus is very smooth. Taste and add extra salt if needed.

Transfer to a serving bowl, drizzle with a little oil, sprinkle with paprika, and serve with veggies (*I used mushrooms, radishes, carrots, cucumbers, mini sweet peppers, yellow squash, snow peas, cherry tomatoes, and asparagus*).

MVP SNACK MIX

In a big paper grocery bag, combine 1 (7 oz.) box Cheez-It® crackers, 1 (8 to 9 oz.) pkg. oyster crackers, 1 (9 oz.) can salted cashews, 1 (7.5 oz.) bag Bugles™ snacks, and 1 (16 oz.) bag small pretzel twists. In a pint mason jar, combine ¾ to 1 cup canola oil, 2 (1 oz.) pkgs. dry ranch dressing mix, and 2 tablespoons dill weed; screw on the lid and shake until well combined.

Drizzle over the cracker combo and roll the bag closed; shake to coat everything. Spread on paper towels to dry at room temperature, or divide among two parchment paper-lined jelly roll pans and bake at 325°F for 10 to 15 minutes, then spread on paper towels to cool. Store in airtight containers.

CHOCOLATE MARSHMALLOW CHEX MIX

🏈 **SERVES A CROWD** 🏈

Line a big work surface with waxed paper. In a big saucepan over medium heat (*or in a really big microwave-safe bowl on 50% power in the microwave*), melt together 1 cup butter, 1 (11.5 oz.) bag milk chocolate chips, and 1 (10 oz.) bag dark chocolate chips; remove from the heat and stir in 1 cup malted milk powder. Quickly stir in 2 (12.8 oz.) boxes Chocolate Chex cereal until coated (*you might need to get in there with your hands to break apart the clumps*).

Spread out on the waxed paper to cool. Then mix in a 10-oz. bag of mini marshmallows and a 10-oz. pkg. malted milk balls until combined. Eat them as is or dump into a brown grocery bag with 2 cups powdered sugar and shake to coat. Or make everybody happy and shake half the Chex mixture with half the powdered sugar and mix together with the plain batch for half-and-half scrumptiousness.

CRUNCH & MUNCH LINEUP

🏈 MAKES ABOUT 10 CUPS 🏈

- ✗ 1 (11 oz.) box mini saltine crackers
- ✗ 3 C. oyster crackers
- ✗ 1½ C. canola oil
- ✗ 1 (1 oz.) pkg. dry ranch dressing mix
- ✗ 3 T. garlic pepper
- ✗ 1 T. red pepper flakes

Dump all the crackers into a big bowl. In a separate bowl, whisk together the oil, dressing mix, garlic pepper, and pepper flakes; pour over the crackers and stir to coat. Stir every 15 minutes until the crackers are well coated and the oil has been absorbed. Spread the crackers out on waxed paper to dry about an hour before serving.

HOLY MOLY GUACAMOLE

🏈 MAKES ABOUT 2 CUPS 🏈

Peel, pit, and dice 3 ripe avocados and toss into a bowl with 1 tablespoon lime juice; mash with a fork to reach the desired consistency (*chunky or creamy—your call*). Stir in ½ teaspoon salt, ½ teaspoon ground cumin, ¼ teaspoon cayenne pepper, 1 tablespoon chopped fresh cilantro, 2 tablespoons finely chopped red onion, 2 Roma tomatoes (*seeded and diced*), ½ jalapeño pepper (*seeded and finely chopped*), and ½ teaspoon minced garlic.

Transfer to a serving bowl and sprinkle with a little black pepper. Serve with tortilla chips or veggies.

HUDDLE UP!

To store for a short time, press plastic wrap directly onto the surface and refrigerate.

REMINDER

Don't forget to grab the Fruit Salsa from the fridge, and make sure you pack a serving spoon—unless you're a fan of double-dipping.

CINNAMON-SUGAR TORTILLA CHIPS & FRUIT SALSA

🏈 SERVES A CROWD 🏈

- ✗ 2 T. sugar
- ✗ 1 T. brown sugar
- ✗ 3 T. fruit preserves, any flavor (*I used raspberry*)
- ✗ 2 kiwis, peeled & diced
- ✗ 2 Golden Delicious apples, diced
- ✗ 1 (6 oz.) pkg. fresh raspberries
- ✗ 1 lb. fresh strawberries, diced
- ✗ 1 C. fresh blueberries
- ✗ 10 (10") flour tortillas
- ✗ Cooking spray
- ✗ Cinnamon-sugar

In a big bowl, mix the sugar, brown sugar, and preserves until well combined. Add the kiwis, apples, raspberries, strawberries, and blueberries; stir to blend. Cover and chill.

Preheat the oven to 350°F. Coat one side of each tortilla with cooking spray. Sprinkle with cinnamon-sugar and spritz again with cooking spray. Cut each tortilla into eight wedges and arrange in a single layer on baking sheets. Bake on the bottom oven rack for 10 to 15 minutes, until lightly browned; cool.

If you're traveling, pack the chips lightly in an airtight container or big zippered plastic bags.

TEQUILA-LIME PINEAPPLE MANGO SALSA

🏈 MAKES 6 CUPS 🏈

- ✗ 2 firm ripe mangoes
- ✗ 1 pineapple, peeled
- ✗ 1 red bell pepper
- ✗ 3 T. melted unsalted butter
- ✗ ⅔ C. chopped red onion
- ✗ ¼ C. chopped fresh cilantro
- ✗ Juice of ½ lime
- ✗ ⅛ tsp. black pepper
- ✗ 1 T. agave nectar
- ✗ 2 T. tequila
- ✗ 1½ tsp. smoked paprika

Slice off the two fat sides of each mango; cut a crisscross pattern into the fruit slices without cutting through the skin. Core the pineapple and cut into six wedges. Cut the bell pepper into thirds; remove the stem and seeds.

Grease the grill rack and preheat the grill on medium heat. Brush the mango, pineapple, and pepper pieces with butter and arrange on the hot grill rack. Cook everything until grill marks appear, flipping the pineapple and pepper to brown all sides. Set all aside to cool.

Use a spoon to remove the mango pieces from the skin; toss the pieces into a bowl. Cut the pineapple and pepper into bite-size pieces and add to the bowl along with the onion, cilantro, lime juice, pepper, agave nectar, tequila, and paprika. Stir until well blended.

Serve with tortilla chips or use as a condiment for grilled burgers.

TEXAS CAVIAR

🏈 MAKES ABOUT 5 CUPS 🏈

- ✗ 1½ T. lime juice
- ✗ 2½ T. olive oil
- ✗ ½ tsp. sea salt
- ✗ ¼ tsp. paprika
- ✗ ¼ tsp. cayenne pepper

- ✗ 1 (15 oz.) can black beans, drained & rinsed
- ✗ 1 diced tomato
- ✗ ¾ C. frozen corn kernels, thawed

- ✗ ½ C. diced red onion
- ✗ 1 diced red bell pepper
- ✗ 2 diced jalapeño peppers
- ✗ 1 avocado
- ✗ Fresh cilantro

- ✗ Good Sport Pita Chips (*recipe on facing page*)

In a bowl, whisk together the lime juice, oil, salt, paprika, and cayenne. Stir in the beans, tomato, corn, onion, bell pepper, and jalapeños. Chill a couple of hours to mingle the flavors.

Just before serving, peel, pit, and dice the avocado and chop up a handful of cilantro; stir both into the chilled bean mixture.

Serve with pita chips.

HUDDLE UP!

If you're hoping your Texas Caviar will last several days, stir the avocado into only what you're serving or leave it out altogether so it doesn't turn brown.

GOOD SPORT PITA CHIPS

🏈 MAKES 40 🏈

Brush olive oil over one side of 5 pita bread rounds; sprinkle with sea salt and coarse black pepper. Add other seasonings if you'd like. Cut each round into eight triangles and bake at 375°F for 10 minutes or until toasted.

TAILGATE TRIVIA

The first "American football game" (pre-dating modern American football rules) was between Princeton and Rutgers in 1869. Some say modern tailgating began at the same time when fans grilled sausages at the "tail-ends" of the horses drawing their carriages.

LOADED QUESO

🏈 SERVES A CROWD 🏈

Brown ½ lb. spicy pork sausage, crumbling it while it cooks; drain and dump into a 2-quart baking dish. Stir in ¾ cup pale ale (*or another favorite*), 16 oz. Velveeta® (*cubed*), ½ cup shredded Pepper Jack cheese, 1 (14.5 oz.) can Mexican seasoned tomatoes (*undrained*), and 1 cup black beans (*drained & rinsed*).

    Bake at 350°F for 30 minutes, or until the cheese is melted and everything is nice and hot. Stir in ¼ cup chopped fresh cilantro. Serve with taco-flavored Doritos.

HUDDLE UP!

To make in a slow cooker, simply toss the browned and drained pork with the other ingredients into a 2-quart cooker; heat on high for 2 to 3 hours. Or heat on the grill by putting the ingredients into a 2-quart disposable foil pan; cover with foil and heat until warm and melty.

MAKE IT A SANDWICH

Eliminate the round bread loaf – no need for that here. Mix all the ingredients except the lettuce as directed above and simply mound the mixture on lettuce-lined hoagie rolls. Super easy. Just as yummy.

HOAGIE DIP

🏈 SERVES 8 🏈

- ✗ 1 medium onion
- ✗ 2 pickled banana peppers
- ✗ ½ head iceberg lettuce
- ✗ 1 big tomato, seeded

- ✗ 1 (3 oz.) pkg. thinly sliced genoa salami
- ✗ 1 (7 oz.) pkg. each thinly sliced honey ham and roasted turkey breast

- ✗ ¼ lb. thinly sliced white cheddar cheese
- ✗ ½ C. mayo
- ✗ 1 T. olive oil
- ✗ 1 tsp. dried oregano
- ✗ 1½ tsp. dried basil

- ✗ ¼ tsp. red pepper flakes
- ✗ 1 (10 to 12") round bread loaf (*I used ciabatta*)
- ✗ 8 hoagie rolls

Chop the onion, peppers, lettuce, tomato, salami, ham, turkey, and cheese and toss into a bowl.

In a separate bowl, whisk together the mayo, oil, oregano, basil, and pepper flakes; add to the meat mixture, stirring until well combined. Chill until ready to serve.

Carve out the center of the round bread loaf, keeping the sides and bottom intact. Pack the meat mixture into the hollowed-out bread. Cut the bread scraps and the hoagie rolls into big chunks.

To serve, mound the dip onto bread chunks and enjoy a mouthful.

BBQ CHICKEN SKILLET DIP

🏈 SERVES A CROWD 🏈

Preheat the grill on medium-low heat. Cut 2 (8 oz.) blocks of cream cheese in half horizontally and set the pieces side by side in a greased 12" cast iron skillet. Dump 1 (15 oz.) can each corn and black beans (*drained and rinsed*) and 2 sliced green onions on the cream cheese. Mix 1 cup sour cream, ½ cup BBQ sauce, 1 teaspoon garlic powder, 6 oz. grilled chicken breast (*or use a 6 oz. pkg. of grilled chicken, like Carving Board brand*), and ½ cup each shredded Pepper Jack and cheddar cheeses; dump over the veggies in the pan and top with a little more cheese.

Set the skillet on the grill, close the lid, and heat 10 to 15 minutes or until the cheese melts and everything is warm. Toss on some chopped red onion and diced avocado and add a drizzle of BBQ sauce. Serve warm with tortilla chips.

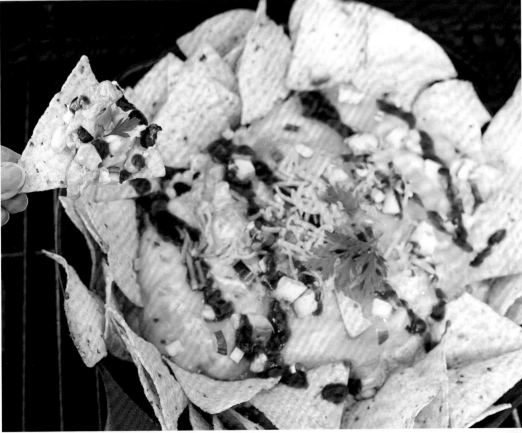

HUDDLE UP!

This recipe makes a lot of dip. Consider dividing into smaller portions and freezing some for later. Then just thaw and dip.

LIME COLADA FRUIT DIP

🏈 MAKES 4 CUPS 🏈

Beat 1 (8 oz.) pkg. cream cheese (*softened*) in a big mixing bowl on medium speed until very creamy. Beat in 1 (14 oz.) can sweetened condensed milk, 1 (6 oz.) container key lime yogurt, 1 (6 oz.) container piña colada yogurt, 1 teaspoon vanilla, and 1 tablespoon lemon juice until light and smooth; stir in the zest and juice of 1 lime.

Cover and refrigerate overnight. Serve with fruit (*I used strawberries, orange segments, and pineapple chunks*).

TAILGATE TRIVIA

When American football first began, touchdowns were only worth four points, while field goals were worth five!

QUESO BLANCO

🏈 MAKES 3 CUPS 🏈

- ✗ 1 (8 oz.) pkg. cream cheese, softened (*not light or fat-free*)
- ✗ ½ lb. each shredded cotija and Pepper Jack cheeses
- ✗ ¾ C. milk, divided
- ✗ 1 (8 oz.) container sour cream (*not light or fat-free*)
- ✗ ¼ tsp. cayenne pepper, or more to taste
- ✗ Tortilla chips

Beat the cream cheese until smooth; dump into a slow cooker. Stir in both shredded cheeses, ½ cup of the milk, the sour cream, and cayenne. Cover and heat on low 2 to 3 hours, until the cheese melts, stirring occasionally. Add the remaining ¼ cup milk if needed. Use a "keep warm" setting for continued dipping. Serve with chips.

CREAMY CRANBERRY SPREAD

🏈 SERVES A CROWD 🏈

- ✗ 1 (12 oz.) pkg. fresh cranberries
- ✗ 1 C. sugar
- ✗ 6 green onions, chopped
- ✗ ⅓ C. chopped fresh cilantro
- ✗ ½ to 1 jalapeño pepper, seeded & finely chopped
- ✗ 1½ (8 oz.) pkgs. cream cheese, softened
- ✗ Your favorite crackers

Dump the cranberries and sugar into a food processor and process briefly until coarsely chopped. Transfer the mixture to a bowl and stir in the green onions, cilantro, and jalapeño. Cover and refrigerate overnight.

After chilling, drain the cranberry mixture. Spread the cream cheese on a plate and spoon the drained mixture over the top. Serve with crackers.

HUDDLE UP!
Use the remainder of the refried beans to make Macho Nacho Dogs, page 72.

TAILGATER'S BEST FIESTA CUPS

🏈 MAKES 6 🏈

Stir together ½ (16 oz.) can refried beans and ½ to 1 (1.25 oz.) pkg. taco seasoning mix until well blended; divide evenly among six 5-oz. cups. Over the bean mixture in each cup, spread a heaping tablespoon each guacamole, sour cream, and salsa.

Sprinkle 1 to 2 tablespoons shredded cheddar cheese over the salsa and top with sliced green onions, sliced black olives, and diced tomatoes; cover and chill until serving time. Serve with tortilla or corn chips.

ORANGE CRANBERRY CHEESE BALL

🏈 SERVES A CROWD 🏈

✘ 1 (8 oz.) pkg. cream cheese, softened
✘ 1 C. powdered sugar
✘ 2½ tsp. orange zest, divided
✘ 1½ tsp. orange juice
✘ ¾ C. dried sweetened cranberries, divided
✘ ½ C. chopped pecans, toasted
✘ Buttery crackers

Beat the cream cheese until smooth. Stir in the powdered sugar, 1 teaspoon orange zest, orange juice, and ½ cup cranberries; chill 30 minutes. Form the mixture into a ball and freeze 30 minutes. Mix the pecans, the remaining 1½ teaspoons zest, and the remaining ¼ cup cranberries. Coat the chilled cheese ball with the pecan mixture. Serve with crackers.

TOUCHDOWN CHEESE BALL

🏈 SERVES A CROWD 🏈

- ✗ 2 (8 oz.) pkgs. cream cheese, softened
- ✗ 1 tsp. Italian seasoning
- ✗ 8 oz. finely shredded mozzarella cheese
- ✗ ½ C. shredded Parmesan cheese
- ✗ 3 green onions, thinly sliced
- ✗ ½ C. chopped cooked bacon
- ✗ 1 (4 oz.) jar diced pimentos, drained
- ✗ 2 (5 oz.) pkgs. mini pepperoni slices, divided
- ✗ 1 slice white cheese (*any kind*)
- ✗ Crackers, pretzels, and/ or breadsticks

Line a small bowl with plastic wrap, letting the ends of the wrap hang over the side of the bowl; set aside.

Beat the cream cheese until light and fluffy. Beat in the Italian seasoning, mozzarella, and Parmesan. Mix in the green onions, bacon, pimentos, and 1 package of the pepperoni. Press the cheese mixture firmly into the bowl and cover with the ends of the plastic wrap. Remove the plastic-covered ball from the bowl and press it into a football shape. Chill at least 2 hours.

Remove the cheese ball from the plastic wrap and let stand 15 minutes. Finish your "football" by covering the cheese ball with more pepperoni slices, pressing to adhere. Cut the slice of cheese into strips and use to decorate the top like football laces. Serve with crackers, pretzels, and/or breadsticks.

PARTY SHRIMP

🏈 SERVES ABOUT 10 🏈

- ✗ 1 (.7 oz.) pkg. dry Italian dressing mix
- ✗ ¼ C. vegetable oil
- ✗ ½ tsp. paprika
- ✗ ½ tsp. garlic powder
- ✗ ¼ tsp. cayenne pepper
- ✗ Pinch of salt
- ✗ 1½ lbs. large shrimp, peeled & deveined (*thawed if frozen*)
- ✗ Cocktail sauce and/or creamy Italian dressing for dipping

Whisk together the dressing mix, oil, paprika, garlic powder, cayenne, and salt until well combined; pour into a big zippered plastic bag and add the shrimp, tossing to coat. Refrigerate a couple of hours.

After the shrimp has chilled, preheat your broiler and arrange the shrimp in a single layer on a rimmed baking sheet (*discard the marinade*). Broil 4" from the heat 5 to 7 minutes, until pink and opaque, flipping once. Serve hot or at room temperature with cocktail sauce and/or dressing.

ALL-STAR PICKLE WRAPS

🏈 MAKES ABOUT 15 🏈

Mix 2 oz. cream cheese (*softened*) with 3 tablespoons mayo until nice and smooth. Stir in ½ cup finely shredded cheddar cheese, ¼ teaspoon garlic powder, and salt and cayenne pepper to taste. Chill for 30 minutes.

Drain 1 (24 oz.) jar Stackers dill pickles and put between layers of paper towels, pressing out as much juice as possible. Spread 1 teaspoon of the chilled cream cheese mixture over each pickle slice. Chop 6 thin slices peppered salami and sprinkle evenly over the cream cheese. Roll up and secure with toothpicks.

BACON & SAUSAGE JALAPEÑO POPPERS

🏈 MAKES 20 🏈

Preheat the grill on medium-low heat. Slice 10 jalapeños in half lengthwise; remove and discard the seeds and membranes. (*You know the drill: Always be careful prepping jalapeños—these beasts can do a number on your skin and eyes.*)

Mix an 8 oz. tub of cream cheese spread with 1 cup finely shredded Monterey Jack cheese, 1 teaspoon chipotle powder, and 2 finely chopped green onions; stuff into the pepper halves.

Nestle a mini smoked sausage into the filling of each and wrap a cooked bacon strip around the whole thing. Secure with toothpicks and set them on the grill; close the lid and cook several minutes, until the peppers are slightly tender and lightly charred and the filling is piping hot.

SPINACH MUSHROOM STARTERS

🏈 MAKES 18 🏈

Preheat the grill on medium heat. Remove the stems and gills from 18 portabellini mushrooms and rub melted butter over the outside of each.

Stir together 1 (8 oz.) pkg. softened cream cheese, 2 cups shredded sharp cheddar cheese, 2½ teaspoons minced garlic, and 4 cups firmly packed chopped fresh spinach. Stuff the cheese mixture evenly into the mushrooms and season with salt and black pepper to taste. Set them on the grill, close the lid, and cook about 10 minutes, until the mushrooms are cooked and the filling is hot and melty.

TAILGATE TRIVIA

The very first NFL draft pick was Jay Berwanger in 1936. He was also the first winner of the Heisman trophy.

BACON-WRAPPED CANTALOUPE SKEWERS

🏈 **SERVINGS VARY** 🏈

Use a melon baller to scoop the fruit from a cantaloupe. Partially cook 1 bacon strip for each melon ball, and drain the bacon on paper towels.

Grease the grill rack and preheat the grill on medium heat. Wrap a partially cooked bacon strip around each melon ball and slide onto skewers, securing the bacon to the melon. Arrange the skewers on the hot grill and let them cook for a few minutes on each side until the bacon gets nice and crispy.

TAILGATE TIP

Tying balloons or flags to your vehicle or tent will make it easier for you, your friends, and your family to find the right party spot!

RADISH CROSTINI

🏈 SERVINGS VARY 🏈

- ✗ 2 lbs. radishes, any variety, trimmed & halved
- ✗ Olive oil
- ✗ Salt & black pepper to taste
- ✗ About 1 lb. sliced whole grain bread
- ✗ Ricotta cheese
- ✗ 1½ C. coarsely chopped arugula
- ✗ ¼ C. lemon juice
- ✗ 1 green onion, finely chopped
- ✗ 2 tsp. honey

Preheat the grill on medium heat. In a bowl, toss radishes with 2 tablespoons oil; sprinkle with salt and pepper and place on a grill pan. Grill the pan of radishes for 8 to 10 minutes or until they're tender and lightly browned, turning occasionally. Remove from the heat and let cool.

Cut the bread slices into smaller pieces, if you'd like. Brush both sides of the bread with oil, and set directly on the grill rack until toasted on the bottom; flip and toast on the other side. Remove from the grill and spread some ricotta on one side of each piece.

Chop the cooled radishes into smaller pieces and toss them into a bowl with the arugula, lemon juice, green onion, honey, and 2 tablespoons oil. Season with more salt and pepper and stir it all up.

Use a slotted spoon to transfer a generous portion of the radish mixture onto each of the toasted bread pieces. Serve immediately.

HUDDLE UP!

Ricotta cheese spreads easily and helps mellow out the robust flavor of the radishes. Spread it as thin or thick as you'd like.

HUDDLE UP!

Stir up the chicken mixture and refrigerate until serving time. Then just core and cut the apples and put these together at the last minute.

CHICKEN SALAD CRISPS

🏈 MAKES ABOUT 12 🏈

Stir together ¼ cup vegetable-flavored cream cheese spread, ¼ cup mayo, 1 tablespoon finely chopped onion, 1 teaspoon apple cider vinegar, 1 teaspoon sea salt, and ½ teaspoon black pepper until creamy. Stir in 1½ cups diced rotisserie chicken, ½ cup chopped celery, and ¼ cup dried sweetened cranberries (*chopped*).

Core 4 apples (*I used Golden and Red Delicious*) and cut into ½" crosswise slices; brush with lemon juice and sprinkle with a bit of sea salt and black pepper. Cut up lettuce into small pieces and lay one piece on each apple slice, then scoop on some of the chicken mixture and top with a pecan half.

JALAPEÑO POPPER BLITZ

🏈 MAKES 6 🏈

Grease the grill rack and preheat the grill on medium-high heat. Stir together 6 oz. softened cream cheese, 1 finely chopped green onion, ½ teaspoon garlic powder, and ⅓ cup shredded Colby Jack cheese.

Cut off but don't discard the stem end from 6 jalapeño peppers; scoop out the seeds. Stuff the cheese mixture into the hollowed-out peppers, packing tightly; replace the stem ends. Wrap one bacon strip around each pepper; run a skewer* lengthwise through the pepper, catching the ends of the bacon and securing them to the pepper.

Cook on the hot rack for 10 minutes, until bacon is crisp and peppers are tender, turning often.

*Soak wooden skewers in water for ½ hour or use metal skewers.

SALTY & SAVORY CANAPÉS

🏈 **MAKES ABOUT 24** 🏈

Toss ½ cup chopped walnuts into a dry skillet and toast over medium heat for 10 minutes, stirring occasionally; let cool. Mix ½ cup chopped & well drained roasted red peppers, 4 chopped green onions, 2 teaspoons olive oil, ½ teaspoon each coarse salt and black pepper; stir in the set-aside toasted walnuts. Serve on sturdy potato chips.

HUDDLE UP!

Canapés [KAN-uh-pays] are typically savory-topped breads, crackers, or pastries, but this potato chip version adds salty crunch and interest.

CUCUMBER CUPS

🏈 **MAKES ABOUT 30** 🏈

Finely chop ½ red bell pepper and 1 tomato and toss into a bowl. Add 2 tablespoons each finely chopped red onion and black olives, 2¼ teaspoons dried oregano, 3 tablespoons crumbled feta cheese, ¼ cup chopped fresh parsley, 1 teaspoon olive oil, the zest of 1 lemon, and 1¼ teaspoons lemon juice. Season with salt and black pepper to taste.

Cut the ends off 2 cucumbers; remove the skin from the cucumbers in thin strips, making a striped pattern if you'd like. Cut the cukes into ½"-thick slices. Using a spoon, make a very shallow divot in the center of each slice, being careful not to push through the bottom. Using a small slotted spoon, scoop the tomato mixture onto the cucumbers.

HUDDLE UP!

Chill the wrapped tortilla rolls several days in advance, then just slice before serving.

CHERRY ROLL-UPS

🏈 MAKES ABOUT 35 🏈

Stir together 1½ cups dried sweetened cherries or dried cherry-flavored cranberries, 2 (8 oz.) pkgs. cream cheese (*softened*), 1½ cups crumbled feta cheese (*not light or fat-free*), and ½ cup chopped green onions (*white and light green parts*) until well mixed. Spread the mixture evenly over 5 (9" to 10") spinach tortillas. Roll up tightly, holding the filling inside, and wrap in plastic wrap. Refrigerate at least 1 hour. After chilling, trim off the ends and cut each roll into 1" slices.

TAILGATE TRIVIA

Around 95% of tailgaters prepare their food at the stadium. The rest bring fast food or premade meals and snacks.

TEX-MEX TORTILLA TWIRLS

🏈 SERVES A CROWD 🏈

- ✗ 6 oz. cream cheese, softened
- ✗ 12 oz. sour cream
- ✗ 2 T. taco seasoning
- ✗ ½ (16 oz.) can refried beans (*I used black bean refried beans*)
- ✗ 8 (10") flour tortillas
- ✗ 1 C. frozen peas, thawed
- ✗ ½ C. shredded carrot
- ✗ ½ C. thinly sliced green onions (*white and light green parts*)
- ✗ 1 (11 oz.) can Mexicorn, well drained
- ✗ 1½ C. finely shredded Mexican cheese blend

Combine cream cheese and sour cream in a mixing bowl and beat until smooth. Mix in taco seasoning until well combined.

Spread some of the refried beans down the middle of each tortilla. Spread the cream cheese mixture on both sides of the beans, leaving about ½" uncovered around the edge of the tortillas. Sprinkle evenly with peas, carrot, green onions, corn, and cheese. Fold in the sides of the tortillas and roll up tightly. Wrap in plastic wrap and chill overnight.

Unwrap the tortillas and use a sharp knife to cut each into 1" slices before serving.

CHAMPION CAPRESE SKEWERS

🏈 **SERVES 8** 🏈

- ✗ ½ C. balsamic vinegar
- ✗ ⅓ C. olive oil
- ✗ 1 clove garlic, thinly sliced
- ✗ ¼ lb. French bread
- ✗ 6 oz. grilling cheese*
- ✗ 16 cherry tomatoes
- ✗ Coarse salt to taste
- ✗ Fresh basil leaves
- ✗ Skewers**

In a small saucepan over medium heat, heat vinegar for 20 minutes or until reduced by half. In a separate saucepan over low heat, heat oil and garlic for 10 minutes. Remove both from the heat; cover reduced vinegar and set aside.

Preheat the grill on high heat. Cut the bread and cheese into 1" cubes. Thread bread cubes, cheese cubes, and cherry tomatoes onto skewers; brush with the hot garlic oil and sprinkle with salt. Set on the grill rack and cook a few minutes, until grill marks appear, turning every minute or so to brown all sides.

At serving time, toss on some basil leaves and serve skewers with the set-aside reduced vinegar.

*Look for halloumi, queso blanco, or other cheese with a high melting point.
**Soak wooden skewers in water for ½ hour or use metal skewers.

GRAPE & THYME APPETIZERS

🏈 SERVINGS VARY 🏈

Preheat the grill on low heat. Stem a couple bunches of purple seedless grapes, cut them in half, and toss in a single layer into a foil pan. Stir in a little olive oil; sprinkle with salt and dried thyme to taste.

Set the pan on the hot grill for 5 to 10 minutes, until the grapes have softened a bit, stirring occasionally. Set aside to cool slightly.

Spread some softened cream cheese on your favorite crackers and top with a little scoop of grapes.

CAJUN NUTS

🏈 MAKES 5 CUPS 🏈

✗ 2 C. unsalted peanuts
✗ 1 C. each unsalted cashews, whole almonds, and pecan halves
✗ 1½ tsp. Cajun seasoning
✗ 2 tsp. sugar
✗ 1 tsp. each salt and coarse black pepper
✗ 2 T. vegetable oil
✗ 1 tsp. minced garlic

Preheat your oven to 200°F. In a big bowl, combine all the nuts. In a small bowl, mix the Cajun seasoning, sugar, salt, and black pepper. In a small skillet, heat the oil over medium heat; add the garlic and cook for a minute, then drizzle over the nuts, tossing to coat. Sprinkle with the spice mixture; toss to coat. Spread out on a rimmed baking sheet and bake for 45 minutes, stirring occasionally.

Cajun Spice

TACO PUFFS

🏈 MAKES 18 🏈

- ✗ 1 (10 oz.) can diced tomatoes with green chiles
- ✗ 1 (17.3 oz.) pkg. frozen puff pastry
- ✗ 1 lb. lean ground beef
- ✗ 1 (1 oz.) pkg. taco seasoning
- ✗ 1 C. shredded Pepper Jack cheese
- ✗ 1 C. shredded cheddar cheese
- ✗ Guacamole and sour cream for serving

Drain the tomatoes with green chiles, collecting the liquid in a 1 cup measuring cup; add enough water to measure ⅔ cup and set aside. Remove the puff pastry from the freezer and let stand at room temperature according to package directions. Cook the ground beef in a big skillet until no longer pink, crumbling it as it cooks; drain and return to the skillet. Stir in the taco seasoning, the drained tomatoes with green chiles, and the set-aside liquid. Bring to a boil, reduce the heat, and simmer until the liquid has nearly evaporated.

Unfold the pastry sheets on a lightly floured work surface. Using a pizza cutter, cut each sheet into nine equal squares. Divide the taco meat and both cheeses among the squares, diagonally across the middle. Wet two opposite corners with water, bring to the center over the filling, and press to seal.

Arrange the puffs on two waxed paper-lined trays and place in the freezer until solid. Once solid, bake immediately or transfer to a freezer bag to bake at a later date. When you're ready to bake, preheat your oven to 400°F. Arrange the frozen puffs on rimmed parchment paper-lined baking sheets. Bake without thawing 20 to 25 minutes, until golden brown. Serve with sour cream and/or guacamole if you'd like.

MAIN DISHES

HUDDLE UP!

These sandwiches will hold up for several hours. If you're going to make these even further ahead than that, leave off the tomatoes and the horseradish sauce and add those at serving time. Wrap the sandwiches in plastic, foil, or parchment paper and use string to hold in place, making it easier to eat; keep chilled.

PICNIC SANDWICHES

🏈 MAKES 6 FULL-SIZE SANDWICHES 🏈

- ✗ ½ C. mayo
- ✗ ½ C. sour cream
- ✗ ¼ C. prepared horseradish
- ✗ ¼ to ½ tsp. lemon zest
- ✗ Coarse salt and black pepper
- ✗ Hot sauce to taste
- ✗ 6 hoagie or steak rolls
- ✗ 3 or 4 tomatoes, sliced
- ✗ 1½ lbs. sliced deli roast beef
- ✗ Lettuce
- ✗ 1 red onion, thinly sliced

Mix the mayo, sour cream, horseradish, lemon zest, and 1¼ teaspoons salt. Season generously with black pepper and hot sauce. Cover and chill at least 30 minutes.

When you're ready to eat, spread the chilled horseradish sauce over the bottom half of the rolls (*or serve it alongside the sandwiches instead*). Add some tomato slices and season with salt and pepper. Top with roast beef, lettuce, and onion. Cut in half for serving.

HIGH-OCTANE CHILI

🏈 MAKES ABOUT 8 CUPS 🏈

- ✗ ½ onion, diced
- ✗ 1 lb. lean ground beef
- ✗ 1 tsp. vegetable oil
- ✗ 1 (6 oz.) can Italian tomato paste
- ✗ 1 (15 oz.) can chili beans

- ✗ 1 (15 oz.) can black beans, drained & rinsed
- ✗ 1 (14 oz.) can fire-roasted tomatoes with garlic
- ✗ 1 (16 oz.) bottle dark beer (*I used porter*)

- ✗ 1 tsp. sugar
- ✗ Salt, black pepper, cayenne pepper, and chili powder to taste
- ✗ Your favorite chili toppings

Cook the onion and beef in hot oil until done, crumbling it while it cooks. Stir in the tomato paste, all the beans, tomatoes, beer, sugar, salt, black pepper, cayenne pepper, and chili powder. Simmer 30 minutes or so, until thick and yummy, or transfer to a slow cooker and let it cook until you're ready to eat.

Load up with your favorite toppings or eat it plain. Either way, it's spectacular!

HUDDLE UP!

Chili is a great tailgating food—it can be prepped hours or even days ahead of time, then chilled and reheated when needed.

PASTA & SUMMER VEGGIES

🏈 SERVES 4 🏈

- ✗ 1½ tsp. minced garlic
- ✗ 1 orange bell pepper, diced
- ✗ 1 medium yellow summer squash, cut into bite-size pieces
- ✗ About 20 cherry tomatoes, halved
- ✗ 3 T. dry white wine
- ✗ ½ tsp. dried thyme, basil, or oregano
- ✗ ¼ C. olive oil, divided
- ✗ Salt and ground peppercorn medley to taste
- ✗ 8 oz. uncooked pasta
- ✗ ½ C. shredded Asiago cheese

Preheat the grill on high heat. Coat a big piece of heavy-duty foil with cooking spray.

In a big bowl, combine the garlic, bell pepper, squash, and tomatoes. Add the wine, dried herbs, and 2 tablespoons oil; season well with salt and peppercorn medley. Stir it all up until well coated and transfer to the prepped foil. Wrap the foil tightly around the vegetables, making sure the edges are well sealed. Toss the packet on the grill and cook about 6 minutes, then flip it over and cook 6 minutes longer.

Meanwhile, cook the pasta according to package directions until just al dente; drain and dump into a big bowl. Carefully open the packet and add veggies to the bowl, along with the remaining 2 tablespoons oil; give it a quick stir. Sprinkle with Asiago to serve.

THAI TURKEY WRAPS

🏈 **MAKES 4 FULL-SIZE WRAPS** 🏈

Dice ¾ lb. grilled and cooled turkey breast and toss into a big bowl. Add 1½ cups coleslaw mix, several thinly sliced and halved radishes, 3 thinly sliced green onions, a handful of chopped fresh cilantro, and a handful of dry-roasted peanuts; toss to combine. In a small bowl, whisk together 3 tablespoons each creamy peanut butter, soy sauce, lime juice, brown sugar, and sesame oil. Whisk in 1½ teaspoons minced garlic, a pinch of red pepper flakes, and salt and black pepper to taste.

Pour the sauce over the cabbage mixture and toss to coat thoroughly. Put a few lettuce leaves on 4 (10") flour tortillas, then divide the chicken mixture evenly over the lettuce. Fold in the sides of the tortillas and roll up. Cut in half to serve.

CHEESY CHICKEN SLIDERS

🏈 **MAKES 10 TO 12** 🏈

- ✗ 1¼ lbs. boneless, skinless chicken breasts
- ✗ 1 (12 oz.) can or bottle plus ½ C. beer (*your favorite*), divided
- ✗ 2 garlic cloves, minced
- ✗ 1 tsp. each salt and black pepper
- ✗ ¼ tsp. Tabasco® sauce
- ✗ 1 lb. Velveeta, cubed
- ✗ Prepared yellow mustard
- ✗ 10 to 12 slider or cocktail buns, split
- ✗ 2 T. chopped fresh chives

Put the chicken, 12 oz. beer, garlic, salt, and black pepper in a 1½-quart slow cooker. Cover and cook on low 6 to 8 hours. (*In a hurry? Cook on high 3 to 4 hours instead.*) Shred the chicken thoroughly and stir back into the juices in the cooker.

In the meantime, for the cheese sauce, pour the remaining ½ cup beer into a separate 1-quart slow cooker. Add the Tabasco and Velveeta. Cover and cook on high 45 to 50 minutes, until melted; stir until smooth. (*You can keep the cheese sauce warm and melty on low for up to 4 hours.*)

Spread mustard on the buns and top with chicken, cheese sauce, and chives.

WALKING TACOS

🏈 MAKES 8 🏈

- ✗ 1 T. butter
- ✗ 1 onion, chopped
- ✗ 2 small jalapeños, seeded & diced
- ✗ 1 lb. ground beef
- ✗ 1 (1 oz.) pkg. taco seasoning mix
- ✗ 1 (14 oz.) can tomato sauce
- ✗ 1 (14 oz.) can kidney beans, drained & rinsed
- ✗ 1 (14 oz.) can diced tomatoes, drained
- ✗ 8 (1 oz.) bags nacho cheese chips
- ✗ Toppings

In a big saucepan over medium heat, melt the butter; add the onion and sauté until just softened. Add the jalapeños and cook 2 to 3 minutes more. Add the ground beef and cook until done, crumbling it while it cooks. Drain, return to the pan, and stir in the taco seasoning.

Dump the tomato sauce, kidney beans, and canned tomatoes into the saucepan with the meat and cook until heated through, stirring occasionally.

Open the bags of nacho cheese chips and let everybody build their own taco by scooping some of the meat mixture into the chip bags and adding toppings of their choice. (I used fresh tomatoes, jalapeños, radishes and sour cream.)

GRILL COOKING

BATTER UP BEER BURGERS

🏈 MAKES 6 🏈

- ✗ 1½ lbs. extra lean ground beef
- ✗ 3 T. finely chopped onion
- ✗ 1 tsp. minced garlic
- ✗ 2 T. Worcestershire sauce
- ✗ ⅓ C. of your favorite beer (*I used chocolate porter*)
- ✗ 1½ tsp. olive oil
- ✗ 1½ tsp. salt
- ✗ Black pepper
- ✗ Butter, softened
- ✗ 6 hamburger buns, split (*I used onion buns*)
- ✗ Mayo
- ✗ Tomato slices

Combine ground beef, onion, garlic, Worcestershire sauce, beer, oil, salt, and ½ teaspoon black pepper and mix gently with your hands. Form six equal patties, press an indentation in the middle of each, and chill for at least an hour.

Grease the cooking grate of a grill and preheat the grill on medium-high heat. Grill the burgers to desired doneness. During the last minute or two of grilling, butter the cut sides of the buns and set them butter side down to toast. Put a pat of butter on each burger as you take it off the grill.

Put a burger and tomato slice on a toasted bun bottom and add a dash of pepper. Slather mayo on the top toasted bun as the finishing touch to this truly delicious burger.

HUDDLE UP!
Freeze water in plastic milk jugs to use as jumbo ice blocks in your cooler.

GRILL COOKING

STUFFED BURGERS

🏈 MAKE 6 🏈

- ✗ Wood chips for smoking
- ✗ 1 T. butter
- ✗ 1 (8 oz.) pkg. sliced white mushrooms
- ✗ 1 red bell pepper, diced
- ✗ ½ C. chopped sweet onion

- ✗ 2 T. steak sauce
- ✗ 4 thick-cut bacon strips, cooked crisp & crumbled
- ✗ 3½ lbs. ground beef
- ✗ 1 beer or soda can for forming patties

- ✗ 12 thick-cut bacon strips, optional
- ✗ Coarse salt & black pepper
- ✗ 12 slices of your favorite cheese (*I used sharp cheddar and Pepper Jack*)

Soak a great big handful of wood chips in water for 30 minutes, then drain. In the meantime, melt the butter in a skillet and sauté the mushrooms, bell pepper, and onion until softened. Stir in the steak sauce and cooked bacon and set aside. Line a rimmed baking sheet with foil and spritz with cooking spray. Form the ground beef into six equal-sized balls and arrange them on the baking sheet.

Clean the outside of the beer or soda can and coat it with cooking spray. Press the can firmly into a meatball to form a cup, pressing the edges of the meat to an even thickness and fixing any cracks; wrap each with two bacon strips, if you'd like, and secure with toothpicks. Remove the can and repeat with the remaining meatballs. Season with salt and black pepper and fill with the mushroom mixture.

Grease the grill grate and preheat the grill to 300°F for indirect cooking. For a charcoal grill, toss a big handful of soaked wood chips directly on hot coals. For a gas grill, place wood chips in a smoker box. (*No smoker box? See DIY smoker pouch instructions, opposite.*) Wait until the wood smokes for 10 minutes before grilling food.

Set the stuffed burgers on the cool side of the grill. Close the grill lid and cook 30 to 45 minutes; top each burger with two cheese slices. Cover and cook 1 to 1½ hours longer until the internal temperature of the meat reaches 160°F, maintaining the grill temperature throughout. Do not flip the burgers.

GRILL COOKING

GAME DAY ITALIAN BURGERS

🏈 **MAKES 8** 🏈

- ✗ 2 lbs. ground beef
- ✗ 1 (3 oz.) pkg. prosciutto, chopped
- ✗ 1 (16 oz.) jar Chicago-style Italian giardiniera, well drained & coarsely chopped, divided
- ✗ 1½ T. Italian seasoning
- ✗ Softened butter
- ✗ 8 ciabatta rolls
- ✗ Garlic pepper
- ✗ 8 slices provolone cheese
- ✗ Pickled banana peppers, drained & sliced
- ✗ Arugula

Grease the grill grate and get the grill good and hot.

In a big bowl, mix the ground beef, prosciutto, ⅔ cup giardiniera, and Italian seasoning (*just use your hands to make it easy*). Shape the mixture into eight patties and press a dimple into the center of each.

Turn the grill heat down to medium. Arrange the patties on the hot grill, close the lid, and cook several minutes on each side, until done to your liking.

Meanwhile, butter the cut sides of the rolls and sprinkle with garlic pepper; toast lightly.

Add a cheese slice to each burger and let it melt. Plop these juicy burgers on the toasted rolls and pile on banana peppers, more of the giardiniera, and some arugula.

GRILL COOKING

SOUTHWEST BURGERS

🏈 SERVES 4 🏈

- ✗ 1 lb. ground turkey
- ✗ 1 C. shredded Mexican cheese blend
- ✗ ¼ C. salsa, plus more for serving
- ✗ ¼ C. crushed tortilla chips
- ✗ ¼ C. thinly sliced green onion
- ✗ 1 tsp. smoked chili powder
- ✗ ½ tsp. garlic salt
- ✗ Melted butter
- ✗ 8 Kaiser rolls
- ✗ Tomato, lettuce & red onion

Grease the grill grate and preheat the grill on medium-high heat.

Toss the ground turkey, cheese, ¼ cup salsa, tortilla chips, green onion, chili powder, and garlic salt in a bowl and mix together lightly. Shape into four ¾"-thick patties and press a dimple into the center.

Grill until the internal temperature of the meat reaches 160°F, turning to brown both sides. During the last minute or two, spread butter over the cut sides of the rolls and grill until lightly toasted.

Serve burgers on the toasted rolls with salsa, tomato, lettuce, and red onion.

GRILL COOKING

GRILL-SMOKED PORK LOIN

🏈 SERVES 8 🏈

- ✗ ½ C. mild-flavored molasses
- ✗ 6 T. C. apple cider vinegar, divided
- ✗ ¼ C. Dijon mustard
- ✗ ¼ C. stone-ground mustard
- ✗ 2 to 2½ lbs. pork tenderloin
- ✗ Salt & black pepper to taste

Mix the molasses, 4 tablespoons of the vinegar, and both mustards in a gallon-size zippered plastic bag. Add the tenderloin, zip closed, turn to coat the meat, and chill 4 hours.

Grease the grill grate and preheat the grill to 250°F for indirect cooking. For a charcoal grill, toss a big handful of soaked wood chips directly on hot coals. For a gas grill, place wood chips in a smoker box. (*For DIY Smoker Pouch directions, see page 72.*) Wait until the wood smokes for 10 minutes before grilling food.

Remove the meat from the bag and reserve the marinade. Sprinkle the meat with salt and pepper; set on the cool side of the grill and close the lid. Cook 1 to 1¼ hours or until the internal temperature of the meat reaches 145°F, checking a couple of times during cooking. (*Each time the lid opens, the temperature drops, so try not to check too often.*)

Pour the reserved marinade into a saucepan; add the remaining 2 tablespoons vinegar, bring to a boil on the grill, and cook until slightly thickened. Cut the meat and serve with the heated sauce.

GRILL COOKING
STEAKS & MUSHROOM STIR-FRY

🏈 SERVES 4 🏈

- ✗ **2 tsp. coarse salt**
- ✗ **½ tsp. dried basil**
- ✗ **½ tsp. black pepper**
- ✗ **½ tsp. ground ginger**
- ✗ **½ tsp. dried minced garlic**
- ✗ **4 (8 oz.) steaks (*I used New York Strip*)**
- ✗ **1 tsp. toasted sesame oil**
- ✗ **2 T. peanut oil**
- ✗ **8 oz. sliced fresh mushrooms (*any kind*)**
- ✗ **2 cloves garlic, thinly sliced**
- ✗ **1½ tsp. finely chopped gingerroot**
- ✗ **¼ C. roasted red bell peppers**
- ✗ **½ C. stir-fry sauce**
- ✗ **¼ tsp. red pepper flakes**
- ✗ **Fresh basil, optional**

Grease the grill grate and preheat the grill on medium heat. Stir together the salt, basil, black pepper, ginger, and minced garlic for a simple but sensational seasoning blend.

Rub the seasoning mixture over both sides of the steaks. Grill the meat until it reaches the perfect doneness for you, flipping once. Pull the steaks off the grill, tent with foil, and set aside.

Set a big sauté pan or wok on the grill to preheat a few minutes. Drizzle in the sesame and peanut oils. Add the mushrooms and cook a few minutes, until they're just becoming tender. Toss in the sliced garlic and gingerroot and cook for another minute or so. Add the roasted peppers, stir-fry sauce, and red pepper flakes.

Spoon the mushroom stir-fry over the top of the steaks and toss on some fresh basil for extra glam.

GRILL COOKING

BUFFALO CHICKEN WITH BLUE CHEESE SLAW

🏈 SERVES 6 🏈

- ✗ 1 C. packed coleslaw mix
- ✗ 1 finely chopped Granny Smith apple
- ✗ 2 finely chopped celery ribs
- ✗ 3 T. crumbled Gorgonzola cheese
- ✗ ¼ C. chopped fresh parsley
- ✗ 1 finely chopped green onion
- ✗ 3 T. olive oil
- ✗ 1½ T. apple cider vinegar
- ✗ ½ tsp. sugar
- ✗ Salt & black pepper to taste
- ✗ 1 C. wing sauce
- ✗ ½ C. unsalted butter, melted
- ✗ ⅓ C. ketchup
- ✗ 6 boneless, skinless chicken breast halves
- ✗ Softened butter
- ✗ 6 hefty buns, split (*I used pretzel rolls*)
- ✗ Ranch dressing

For the slaw, combine coleslaw mix, apple, celery, cheese, parsley, and green onion. Stir together oil, vinegar, sugar, salt, and black pepper; add to the slaw, stir to blend, and chill until serving time.

In a big zippered plastic bag, mix the wing sauce, melted butter, and ketchup; remove ½ cup and set aside. Add the chicken to the bag and toss to coat. Marinate at least 30 minutes.

Grease the grill grate and preheat the grill on medium heat. Toss the chicken on the grill (*discard the marinade left in the bag*) and cook until the internal temperature reaches 165°F, turning to brown both sides.

Spread softened butter on the cut sides of the buns and grill until lightly toasted. Set the chicken on the buns; drizzle with ranch dressing and load on the slaw.

LOADED SALMON PATTIES

🏈 SERVES 4 TO 5 🏈

- ✗ 1 (14.75 oz.) can salmon, drained & flaked
- ✗ 2 finely chopped green onions
- ✗ ½ C. finely diced red bell pepper
- ✗ 2 T. chopped fresh parsley
- ✗ 1 lightly beaten egg
- ✗ 2 T. lemon juice
- ✗ ¼ C. panko bread crumbs
- ✗ Sea salt & coarse black pepper to taste
- ✗ Guacamole

Mix the salmon, green onions, bell pepper, parsley, egg, lemon juice, bread crumbs, salt, and black pepper. Form into eight to ten (½" thick) firm patties; freeze for 15 minutes or chill for ½ hour.

Set a grill pan on the grill and preheat on medium or medium-high heat. Coat the pan heavily with cooking spray.

Add the chilled patties. Hear them sizzle? That's a good thing. Heat about 5 minutes on each side, flipping carefully when grill marks appear and the patties hold their shape. Top with some guacamole.

GRILL COOKING

SOUTHERN DRUMSTICKS

🏈 MAKES 12 🏈

- ✗ ¼ C. brown sugar
- ✗ 2 tsp. minced garlic
- ✗ 4 tsp. salt
- ✗ 2 tsp. black pepper
- ✗ 12 chicken drumsticks
- ✗ ½ C. of your favorite sweet BBQ sauce
- ✗ 3 T. pure maple syrup
- ✗ 2 T. ketchup

In a zippered plastic bag, mash together the brown sugar, garlic, salt, and black pepper to form a paste. Toss in the drumsticks, seal the bag, and rub thoroughly until the chicken is coated. Chill overnight.

Grease the grill grate and preheat the grill on medium heat for indirect cooking. Whisk together the BBQ sauce, syrup, and ketchup and set aside.

Arrange the drumsticks on the hot side of the grill, cooking until browned on all sides. Then move them over to the cool side and cook 30 minutes longer, until the internal temperature of the chicken reaches 165°F, basting with the sauce several times near the end of cooking.

GRILL COOKING

TURKEY-APPLE MEATBALLS

🏈 SERVES 8 🏈

Grease the grill grate and preheat the grill on low heat. In a saucepan, whisk together 1 cup BBQ sauce, ½ cup grape jelly, 4 teaspoons apple cider vinegar, and ½ cup chicken stock. Set the saucepan on the grill to slowly warm up.

Shred 2 unpeeled red apples onto heavy-duty paper towels and squeeze out the excess juice; dump the apples into a bowl. Add ½ lb. finely chopped, uncooked bacon, 2 lbs. ground turkey, and 1½ teaspoons salt; mix with your hands until evenly combined.

Use a 2" cookie scoop to form meatballs and thread onto side-by-side thick skewers. Grill 35 to 45 minutes, until cooked through, turning and drizzling with the warmed sauce occasionally. Serve the remaining sauce with the meatballs.

GRILL COOKING

PORK POPS & TOASTED MELON

🏈 SERVES 4 🏈

In a big bowl, mix 1 teaspoon minced garlic, a small handful of chopped cilantro, 1½ teaspoons white pepper, ¼ cup fish sauce, 1 tablespoon soy sauce, ½ cup cream of coconut, 1 tablespoon vegetable oil, and 1 tablespoon sugar. Cut 1 lb. pork tenderloin into long, thin strips; add to the bowl and set aside at least ½ hour. Set a grill pan on the grill and preheat on medium heat.

Weave the marinated pork strips onto skewers and grill 5 to 8 minutes or until cooked through, turning once. Push fresh cantaloupe and watermelon chunks on side-by-side skewers, brush with oil, and sprinkle with salt and white pepper; toss on the grill for a few minutes. Serve immediately.

GRILL COOKING

PERFECT SPIRAL DOGS

🏈 SERVINGS VARY 🏈

Push a long skewer through the length of a hot dog. Starting at one end of the dog, use a sharp knife to make a diagonal cut until your knife rests on the skewer. Make one long continuous spiral cut all around the hot dog through the other end, turning the dog as you go.

Remove the skewer and grill the dog. Place in a bun and fill the nooks and crannies with condiments! A fun new trick for your dog!

TAILGATE TRIVIA

The first televised football game was in 1939. It was watched on around 500 TV sets.

GRILL COOKING

TRADE-WORTHY TACOS

🏈 MAKES 8 🏈

- ✗ 2 tsp. minced garlic
- ✗ 1 jalapeño, finely chopped
- ✗ A handful of fresh cilantro, chopped
- ✗ Juice of 2 limes
- ✗ Juice of 1 orange
- ✗ 2 T. distilled white vinegar
- ✗ ½ C. olive oil
- ✗ Coarse salt & black pepper to taste
- ✗ 2 lbs. steak (*I used Top of Iowa Sirloin*)
- ✗ 8 small flour or corn tortillas
- ✗ Cooking spray
- ✗ Avocado Pico de Gallo (*recipe on page 87*)
- ✗ Toppings of your choice

Mix the garlic, jalapeño, cilantro, lime juice, orange juice, vinegar, oil, salt, and black pepper in a big zippered plastic bag; add the steak, zip closed, and chill for a few hours.

Grease the grill grate and preheat the grill on low heat. Grill the steak until done to your liking, turning once. Take the meat off the grill (*but don't turn off the heat*) and let it stand 5 minutes before slicing across the grain into bite-size pieces. Coat one side of the tortillas with cooking spray and lay them on the grill for a minute or so until warm and pliable.

Load the tortillas with steak, Avocado Pico de Gallo, and any other taco fixings you like.

AVOCADO PICO DE GALLO

Makes about 2½ cups

Chop a pint of cherry tomatoes (*about 24*) and toss them into a bowl with ⅓ cup diced red onion, 3 tablespoons chopped fresh cilantro, 2 tablespoons lime juice, and 1 tablespoon olive oil. Stir in 1 peeled and diced avocado and season with salt and black pepper. Serve with chips, over grilled meat, or on tacos. So colorful. So simple.

MAIN DISHES

GRILLED VEGGIE TACOS

🏈 MAKES 12 🏈

- ✗ 12 soft flour or corn tortillas
- ✗ Olive oil
- ✗ Juice of 3 limes, divided
- ✗ 3 zucchini
- ✗ 2 red onions, peeled
- ✗ 8 oz. whole mushrooms
- ✗ About 20 cherry tomatoes
- ✗ 2 green bell peppers
- ✗ 3 ears sweet corn, husks & silk removed
- ✗ 2 avocados
- ✗ Taco seasoning to taste
- ✗ Salt & black pepper to taste

Preheat the grill and a grill pan on medium-high heat. Brush one side of each tortilla with oil and lime juice, and stack one on top of the other. Wrap the stack in damp paper towels.

Unwrap the tortillas a few at a time and set them on the hot grill pan for a minute or two, until they begin to brown. As you remove each one, gently fold it in half without forcing it closed. Set aside.

Cut the zucchini and onions into ½"-thick slices. Put the zucchini into a bowl with the mushrooms and tomatoes; drizzle with a little oil and toss until everything is coated. Brush the onions, peppers, and sweet corn with oil. Cut the avocados in half lengthwise, remove the pits, and brush the cut sides with lime juice and oil.

Place all the veggies on the hot grill pan or grill rack and sprinkle generously with taco seasoning, salt, and pepper. Grill everything until evenly browned, turning occasionally, and removing each vegetable from the grill when it's tender.

Cut the corn kernels off the ears. Scoop the avocado halves out of their skin and dice them. Coarsely chop all the other grilled veggies. Fill tortilla shells, drizzle with some lime juice, and enjoy! Top with salsa, sour cream, shredded cheese, or anything else you like on your tacos.

GRILL COOKING

DOG PILE

🏈 **SERVINGS VARY** 🏈

Start by grilling your favorite dogs over medium or medium-high heat—light to dark char, your choice. Score bonus points for grilling the buns. Now, step up your game with mind-blowing toppings for doggie heaven deliciousness!

CHIP & DIP DAWGS

Put the grilled hot dogs in those nicely toasted buns. Then add a big mound of French Onion dip, a handful of chopped red onion, and some coarsely crushed potato chips. Be warned—you may have the urge to chase your tail. **Yeah, they're THAT good!**

MACHO NACHO DOGS

Spread refried beans on grilled buns, add grilled hot dogs, shredded longhorn cheese, chopped onion, and pickled or fresh jalapeño slices. Set on foil and return to the grill; close the lid and heat until the cheese melts. Remove from the grill and hit 'em with sour cream and chopped tomato. **Howlin' delicious!**

JACKED-UP PUPS

Grill hot dogs on one side and remove from the grill. Flip 'em over and slice lengthwise, without cutting all the way through. Stuff with shredded Colby Jack cheese. Set on foil and finish grilling cheese side up, until the cheese is melty. Put dogs in grilled buns, top with BBQ sauce, yellow mustard, diced avocado, chopped cooked bacon, and more cheese. **Yip-Yip-Yippee!**

Chip & Dip Dawgs

Macho Nacho Dogs

Jacked-Up Pups

GRILL COOKING

UNDERDOGS

🏈 **MAKES 8** 🏈

- ✗ Olive oil
- ✗ 3 poblano peppers
- ✗ 2 to 3 T. of your favorite mustard (*I used whole grain*)
- ✗ 1 to 2 T. chopped onion
- ✗ 1 to 2 T. salsa
- ✗ Black pepper to taste
- ✗ 1 (16 oz.) can refried beans (*any variety*)
- ✗ 16 (8") flour tortillas
- ✗ 1 (16 oz.) pkg. shredded Colby Jack cheese
- ✗ 8 (¼ lb.) hot dogs
- ✗ Cheese dip, sour cream & salsa

Grease the grill grate and preheat the grill on high heat.

Drizzle oil over the peppers and set them on the hot grill, cooking until they're nicely charred, turning occasionally. Remove and discard the skin, leaving some of the char in place; coarsely chop the peppers, discarding seeds.

Mix the mustard, onion, salsa, black pepper, and beans together and spread evenly over one side of each tortilla. Divide the cheese and chopped peppers over the beans on half the tortillas and stack those on top of the remaining ones, bean sides up; set aside.

Heat the hot dogs on the grill until they're cooked the way you like them. Remove them from the grill but don't turn off the heat. Place a grilled dog on each of the tortilla stacks and roll up to enclose that puppy tightly inside. Spritz the roll-ups with cooking spray and set them on the grill until they have nice grill marks all around, turning as needed.

Set out cheese dip, sour cream, and salsa for dipping.

BEER TUB BRATS

🏈 SERVES 12 🏈

- ✗ 3 (12 oz.) cans beer (*your favorite kind*)
- ✗ 2 yellow onions, sliced
- ✗ 2 tsp. minced garlic
- ✗ ¼ C. butter, cut up
- ✗ 12 brats
- ✗ 12 brat buns
- ✗ Make-Ahead Kraut (*recipe below*)

Set a 9 x 13" foil pan on the grill and add the beer, onions, garlic, and butter. Preheat the grill on medium heat and let the onions cook at least 15 minutes.

Toss the brats on the grill grate alongside the pan and heat until they're thoroughly cooked and browned. Put the cooked brats into the beer mixture to keep warm and moist until serving.

To make it easy for serving, set everything by the grill; put the brats on buns and pile on those beer-infused onions and a load of kraut.

MAKE-AHEAD KRAUT

Makes about 10 cups

In a big bowl, mix 2 (32 oz.) jars sauerkraut (*drained*), 4 celery ribs (*sliced*), 1 each red and green bell pepper (*diced*), and ½ yellow onion (*diced*). Whisk together 2 cups sugar, 2 cups distilled white vinegar, ½ cup vegetable oil, and ½ teaspoon salt and stir into the veggies. Cover and chill 24 hours to let those amazing flavors blend. Everybody needs a good kraut recipe, and this is it!

GRILL COOKING

STEAK & VEGGIE KABOBS

🏈 SERVES 6 TO 8 🏈

- ✗ ½ C. soy sauce
- ✗ ¼ C. rice wine vinegar
- ✗ 3 T. honey
- ✗ 1 T. toasted sesame oil
- ✗ 4 cloves garlic
- ✗ 2 lbs. flank or sirloin steak, trimmed
- ✗ 3 big bell peppers, any color
- ✗ 1 big red onion
- ✗ Coarse salt and black pepper

If you'll be using wooden skewers, soak them in water overnight.

Put the soy sauce, vinegar, honey, oil, and garlic in a gallon-size zippered bag; close and squeeze to combine, then remove about ¼ cup and put in a separate container for later. Cut the steak into 1½ to 2" chunks and add them to the bag; chill for 1 to 8 hours.

Preheat a grill on medium-high heat. Cut the bell peppers and onion into 1½ to 2" chunks and slide onto skewers alternately with the marinated steak chunks. Brush some of the marinade from the bag over the food, season with salt and black pepper, and grill until they're done to your liking, turning occasionally.

After removing from the grill, let the skewers rest for 5 minutes, then brush with the marinade you set aside earlier.

GRILL COOKING

SPICY CITRUS CHICKEN SKEWERS

🏈 SERVES 6 🏈

- ✗ 6 boneless, skinless chicken thighs
- ✗ 3 to 4 chipotle peppers in adobo sauce
- ✗ ½ C. orange juice
- ✗ ¼ C. lime juice
- ✗ 2 T. canola oil
- ✗ 1 tsp. garlic salt
- ✗ 1 to 2 T. hot chili powder
- ✗ 1 tsp. whole black peppercorns
- ✗ Salt to taste
- ✗ 2 or 3 limes, optional

If you'll be using wooden skewers, soak them in water overnight.

Depending on the size and shape of the chicken thighs, push two or three skewers through each thigh, leaving at least 1" between skewers. Set them in a single layer in a big rimmed pan.

Finely chop the chipotle peppers and toss them into a bowl. Whisk in the orange and lime juices, oil, garlic salt, chili powder, and peppercorns. Pour the mixture over the chicken, cover, and refrigerate 1 to 4 hours.

Line the grill grate with foil and spritz with cooking spray; preheat the grill to medium-high. Remove the chicken from the marinade and sprinkle with salt. Grill until golden brown on both sides and cooked through (165°F), turning once. Remove from the grill and let rest 5 minutes. In the meantime, cut the limes in half and grill until marked if you'd like; squeeze their juice over the chicken. Cut each thigh between the skewers, creating individual pieces and making them super easy to grab and eat. Remove the peppercorns before eating.

QUICK SHRIMP SKEWERS

🏈 SERVES 4 TO 5 🏈

- ✗ 3 to 4 T. orange marmalade
- ✗ ½ C. pineapple juice
- ✗ ½ C. coconut milk*
- ✗ 2 to 3 tsp. soy sauce
- ✗ Coarse black pepper
- ✗ 1 lb. extra large shrimp (*about 20*), peeled and deveined
- ✗ Fresh pineapple, peeled & cut into 1" chunks

*The leftover milk can be frozen in ice cube trays and used in smoothies or other recipes.

In a big bowl, stir together the marmalade, pineapple juice, coconut milk, soy sauce, and a healthy shake of black pepper. Toss in the shrimp and set aside.

Grease the grill grate and preheat the grill on medium-low heat.

Push the shrimp and pineapple chunks alternately onto skewers and hit them again with black pepper. Grill a few minutes on each side or until the shrimp are cooked through and everything has nice grill marks, brushing with marinade while cooking.

HUDDLE UP!

Pair foods the same size and with the same cooking times if you're putting them together on a skewer.

Eliminate flaming bamboo skewers by wrapping foil around the portion without food or simply laying that portion over a piece of foil.

GRILL COOKING

CITRUS-SALMON SKEWERS

🏈 SERVES 4 🏈

- ✗ 3 lemons, divided
- ✗ 2 T. chopped fresh parsley
- ✗ 3 cloves garlic, minced
- ✗ 1½ tsp. Dijon mustard
- ✗ ½ tsp. salt
- ✗ ⅛ tsp. black pepper
- ✗ 2 T. canola oil, plus more for brushing
- ✗ 1 to 1½ lbs. salmon fillets, cut into 1" pieces

Grease the grill grate and preheat the grill on medium-low heat. Juice one of the lemons and pour the juice into a bowl. Stir in the parsley, garlic, mustard, salt, pepper, and 2 tablespoons oil; set aside.

Thinly slice the remaining two lemons. Slide the salmon pieces and lemon slices alternately onto four sets of side-by-side skewers (*fold the lemon slices in half*). Brush both sides with the mustard mixture.

Set a piece of foil on the grill grates and brush with oil; arrange the skewers on the foil and cook until the salmon is done, turning once.

BBQ BRAT PIZZAS

🏈 MAKES 6 🏈

Toss 3 or 4 precooked brats or smoked sausages on the grill until heated through and as charred as you like. Take 'em off the grill and cut into slices. Remove the six rolls from a 10 oz. pkg. of frozen cheese ciabatta rolls (*they can be thawed first or used frozen*) and set cheese side up on a foil-lined grill grate. Grill over low heat until heated through.

Remove from the heat and spread with your favorite BBQ sauce. Top with shredded mozzarella cheese, the grilled brat slices, roasted red peppers (*drained and sliced*), and chopped pickles (*dill or sweet*). Return them to the grill, close the lid, and heat until the cheese melts.

GRILL COOKING

CHICKEN ALFREDO PIZZAS

🏈 SERVES 4 🏈

- ✗ 2 C. bread flour
- ✗ 1½ tsp. sugar
- ✗ 1 (.25 oz.) pkg. active dry yeast
- ✗ ¾ tsp. salt
- ✗ ¾ C. warm water (110°F)
- ✗ Olive oil
- ✗ ½ (14.5 oz.) jar Alfredo sauce (*I used roasted garlic parmesan*)
- ✗ 2 Roma tomatoes, finely diced
- ✗ 1 green bell pepper, finely diced
- ✗ ½ small onion, finely diced
- ✗ 6 oz. chicken breast, grilled*
- ✗ 1 C. finely shredded mozzarella cheese
- ✗ ½ C. baby spinach, chopped
- ✗ Grated Parmesan cheese
- ✗ Coarse black pepper

Or use 1 (6 oz.) pkg. grilled chicken like Carving Board brand.

Stir together the flour, sugar, yeast, and salt in the bowl of a stand mixer. Using a dough hook with the mixer running, add the water and 1 tablespoon plus 1 teaspoon oil, and beat until the dough forms a ball. Continue to beat for 5 minutes, until the dough is nice and smooth; transfer to an oiled bowl, cover with plastic wrap, and let rest for 20 minutes. You can use the dough now or chill up to 24 hours (*then let warm to room temperature before rolling out*).

Preheat the grill on low heat. Flatten the dough into a large rectangle on a floured flat cookie sheet, then transfer to a well-greased grill pan, patting to fit. Score with a knife into four rectangles. Cook until the bottom is nicely browned and the dough is firm enough to flip. Remove the pan from the grill, cut dough on the score lines, and flip the dough over.

Brush the edges of the crusts with oil. Spread sauce to within ½" of the edges. Divide the tomatoes, bell pepper, onion, chicken, mozzarella, and spinach among the crusts and sprinkle liberally with Parmesan and black pepper.

Return the pan to the grill, close the lid, and heat until the dough is cooked, the cheese is melted, and everything is nice and warm.

◀81

GRILL COOKING

BACON-AVOCADO PIZZAS

🏈 MAKES 4 🏈

- ✗ 4 artisan thin flatbread pizza crusts (*I used Flatout Spicy Italian for addictive, intense heat*)
- ✗ Olive oil
- ✗ ½ C. tomato sauce
- ✗ 1½ C. each shredded cheddar and provolone cheeses
- ✗ 6 bacon strips, cooked & chopped
- ✗ 1 or 2 Roma tomatoes, very thinly sliced
- ✗ Red onion, finely chopped
- ✗ 2 avocados, seeded, peeled & diced

Make sure all your toppings are ready and setting by the grill, then preheat the grill on low heat.

Drizzle the crusts with oil and set them oil-side down on the grill for a couple of minutes, until grill marks appear. Flip them over onto a flat cookie sheet and spread each with about 2 tablespoons of the sauce. Divide half the cheese among the crusts. Top each with the bacon, tomato, onion, and avocado, and sprinkle the remaining cheese over all.

Slide the pizzas onto the grill and cook several minutes, until the cheese is melted and grill marks appear on the bottom. Serve hot.

GRILL COOKING
BEER-CHEESEWICHES

🏈 MAKES 6 🏈

Preheat the grill on low heat. Stir together 3 cups shredded sharp cheddar cheese, 1 cup shredded Swiss cheese, 1 tablespoon Worcestershire sauce, 1 teaspoon dry mustard, ¼ teaspoon cayenne pepper, and ¼ teaspoon salt. Slowly stir in about ½ (12 oz.) bottle of Pilsner, until the cheese is just barely moistened.

Divide the cheese mixture among 6 slices of Texas toast; spread evenly but not all the way to the edges. Put another slice of bread over the cheese and squish together. Spread a little melted butter over both sides of the sandwiches and arrange on the grill. Close the lid, but don't walk away. In just a couple of minutes, peek at the bottom. When you see golden brown, flip and repeat. Enjoy immediately, but watch out for the molten cheese flow.

SET IT UP

Whip up a variety of taco meats and dump into separate bowls (*I used foil loaf pans set into a 9 x 13" dish*). Set the table with tons of toppings and let everybody build their own taco favorites.

TACO SPREAD

SERVES 8

FISH TACOS

Mix 6 tablespoons tequila, 2 tablespoons vegetable oil, ¼ cup lime juice, 4 teaspoons lime zest, a 2" piece of fresh ginger (*peeled & minced*), 2 teaspoons minced garlic, 2 teaspoons each salt and sugar, 1 teaspoon ground cumin, and ½ teaspoon each cinnamon and black pepper; add 2 lbs. tilapia fillets, flip to coat, and chill 1 hour. Grill the fillets on greased foil over low heat, until the fish flakes easily.

BORDER CHICKEN

Mix ¼ cup taco seasoning, ½ cup lime juice, and a handful of chopped fresh cilantro. Pour the mixture evenly over 2 lbs. boneless, skinless chicken thighs and chill ½ hour. Grill over medium-low heat until done; shred and serve.

START HERE FOR INSPIRATION

The Foundation
Flour tortillas
Crisp taco shells
Taco salad shells
Corn chips
Tortilla chips

Fantastic Finishes
Lime vinaigrette (*for fish tacos*)
Malt vinegar (*for fish tacos*)
Lime wedges
Fresh cilantro

Tantalizing Toppers

Black beans	Lettuce	Cheese sauce
Black olives	Cabbage	Avocado Pico de
Corn kernels	Green onions	Gallo (*page 87*)
Jalapeños	Cheese	Salsa
Tomatoes	Sour cream	Taco Sauce

MAIN DISHES

CORNERBACK CROISSANTS

🏈 **SERVINGS VARY** 🏈

For each sandwich, split a croissant in half horizontally and spread some cherry preserves on the cut sides. Pile on sliced deli ham and add slices of Swiss and Gruyère cheeses. Put the top of the croissant over the cheese and bundle it up in foil. Place on a warm grill for 10 to 15 minutes or until heated through.

GRILL COOKING

BIG BITE SANDWICHES

🏈 MAKES 6 🏈

- ✗ 1 eggplant, sliced ⅜" thick
- ✗ Coarse salt
- ✗ ⅔ C. olive oil
- ✗ 2 tsp. minced garlic
- ✗ 2 bell peppers, any color
- ✗ 2 yellow summer squash, sliced ½" thick
- ✗ 1 red onion, sliced ½" thick
- ✗ 8 oz. whole mushrooms
- ✗ Coarse black pepper
- ✗ 12 (½"-thick) slices ciabatta bread
- ✗ Italian salad dressing
- ✗ 12 slices provolone cheese
- ✗ Fresh spinach
- ✗ 3 large tomatoes, sliced
- ✗ Fresh basil

Preheat the grill on medium-high heat. Sprinkle both sides of eggplant slices with salt and set on a wire rack for 20 minutes; pat dry. Mix the oil and garlic and brush some all over the peppers; set on the hot grill rack until blistered on all sides, turning occasionally. Transfer to a zippered plastic freezer bag; seal and set aside.

Brush eggplant, squash, onion, and mushrooms with the remaining oil; sprinkle with salt and pepper. Arrange veggies on the grill and cook 10 minutes or until grill marks appear on both sides, flipping once. Remove from the grill; slice the mushrooms. Remove the charred skin from the set-aside peppers; cut into strips and remove seeds.

Coat both sides of the bread slices with cooking spray, arrange on the grill, and cook until the bottoms are toasted; flip, drizzle with salad dressing, top each with a provolone slice, and toast the other side. Layer half the bread slices with grilled veggies, spinach, tomatoes, and basil; top with another bread slice.

FOIL PACKS

CLASSIC FOIL PACK DINNER

🏈 SERVINGS VARY 🏈

The secret to successful foil pack cooking? A leak-proof pouch that locks in moisture and flavor. Place your food in the center of a large piece of foil and then wrap it up in one of two ways:

1. Make a **tent pack** to cook vegetables, fruits, the Classic Play Foil Pack Dinner, and other combination packs that need lots of steam but less browning.

2. Make a **flat pack** to cook meat, fish, and other foods that need less steam and more browning.

heavy-duty aluminum foil (don't skimp!)

layer food in the center

butter (or add extra flavor with a little creamed soup or barbeque sauce)

carrots (celery, corn & green beans are good, too)

potatoes

salt & pepper (& other favorite seasonings)

onion (for flavor & moisture)

ground beef patty

TENT PACK
Leave space above food for air to circulate.

FLAT PACK
Press the foil flat against the food.

1. Bring the foil edges together on top. Fold over and crease well.

2. Then roll the top edge down a couple of times and pinch together tightly. Leave some space above food for air to circulate.

3. Lastly, roll up each end to seal both types of packs.

4. Set the hobo pack on hot coals or medium- high heat on a grill for 25 to 30 minutes, until meat is done and vegetables are tender. Rotate the pack several times during cooking. Open carefully and dig in!

LASAGNA FOIL PACK

🏈 SERVES 4 TO 8 🏈

✗ 1 lb. ground sausage
✗ 1 C. chopped mushrooms
✗ ½ C. chopped onion
✗ 1 lb. fresh mozzarella cheese, thinly sliced
✗ ½ C. shredded Parmesan cheese, plus more for serving
✗ ½ tsp. red pepper flakes
✗ 1 tsp. minced garlic
✗ Salt & pepper to taste
✗ Olive oil
✗ 3 tomatoes, thinly sliced, plus more for serving
✗ 12 no-boil lasagna noodles, divided
✗ ½ (6 oz.) pkg. baby spinach
✗ Fresh basil

Cook sausage, mushrooms, and onion in a skillet; let cool. In a bowl, combine both cheeses and all seasonings; drizzle with 2 tablespoons oil and toss well. Sprinkle tomatoes with salt and pepper.

Stack two long pieces of foil together and drizzle oil down the center of top piece. Set one noodle lengthwise on foil and sprinkle evenly with 1 tablespoon water. Repeat the process for three more foil packs. Use half each of the spinach, sausage mixture, tomatoes, and cheese mixture to make one layer of each ingredient on the noodles. Top each with a second noodle and sprinkle with 1 tablespoon water. Repeat layers with remaining filling ingredients. Set a third noodle on each stack; coat with 1 tablespoon water and drizzle with oil. Wrap foil around food to make four flat packs and cook as directed. Before serving, top with more sliced tomatoes, Parmesan cheese, and some snipped basil.

COOKING METHODS

 Set foil packs on the grate over indirect medium heat and cover grill. Cook 10 minutes; flip packs over and cook about 10 minutes more. Let rest 5 minutes before opening.

 Set foil packs on a few hot coals surrounded by more heat. Cook 10 to 15 minutes. Flip packs over and cook 10 to 15 minutes more. Let rest 5 minutes before opening.

HUDDLE UP!

Transfer any leftovers to an airtight container. Spicy and acidic foods can cause foil to become pitted after an extended time.

FOIL PACKS

JAMBALAYA

🏈 SERVES 4 🏈

- ✗ 1 lb. raw medium shrimp, peeled & cleaned
- ✗ 6 to 8 oz. Andouille pork sausage, thinly sliced
- ✗ 1 (14.5 oz.) can diced tomatoes with garlic & olive oil
- ✗ 2 tsp. dried minced onion
- ✗ 4 C. cooked rice
- ✗ 1 green bell pepper, cored & diced
- ✗ 3 to 4 tsp. Cajun seasoning
- ✗ 1 tsp. hot pepper sauce

In a large bowl, toss together the shrimp, sausage, tomatoes, onion, cooked rice, bell pepper, Cajun seasoning, and pepper sauce. Divide the mixture among four large pieces of sprayed foil. Wrap foil around food to make four tent packs, sealing well. Cook as directed.

COOKING METHODS

Set foil packs on the grate over medium-high heat and cover grill. Cook 8 to 10 minutes or until shrimp are pink and everything is heated through.

Set foil packs on hot coals and cook 10 to 15 minutes, rotating once, until shrimp are pink and everything is heated through.

FOIL PACKS
CITRUS VEGGIE FOIL PACK

🏈 SERVINGS VARY 🏈

- ✗ 1 lb. green and/or yellow wax beans
- ✗ 1 lb. cherry tomatoes
- ✗ 1 orange bell pepper, sliced
- ✗ 1 tsp. each coarse salt & black pepper
- ✗ 3 T. grapeseed oil, divided
- ✗ 1 lemon, halved, divided
- ✗ 1 T. each chopped fresh parsley & chives
- ✗ 1 tsp. dried tarragon

Preheat the grill on medium heat. Dump the beans, tomatoes, and bell pepper into a bowl and add the salt, pepper, and 2 tablespoons oil; toss to coat. Transfer the mixture to a large piece of heavy-duty foil. Cut one lemon half into slices and arrange on top of the vegetables. Wrap the foil around the vegetables, folding up the edges to create a packet and leaving space inside for air circulation.

Place the packet on the grill, close the lid, and cook for 15 to 20 minutes or until just tender. Open carefully to avoid steam. Drizzle the remaining 1 tablespoon oil over the top, and sprinkle with the parsley, chives, and tarragon. Squeeze the juice from the other lemon half over all.

FOIL PACKS

TACO-TATER MEAL

🏈 SERVES 4 🏈

- ✗ 1 lb. lean ground beef or turkey
- ✗ 2 T. taco seasoning
- ✗ ¼ C. milk
- ✗ 3 C. frozen diced hash browns, thawed
- ✗ Salt & pepper to taste
- ✗ 1 C. cheese salsa dip
- ✗ Tomato salsa

In a bowl, combine meat, taco seasoning, and milk; mix well. Lightly shape into four even patties. Place each patty in the center of a large piece of sprayed foil. Spread an equal amount of hash browns over each meat patty and sprinkle with salt and pepper. Spoon ¼ cup cheese dip over each serving. Wrap foil around food to make four tent packs. Cook as directed.

COOKING METHODS

Set foil packs on the grate over medium heat and cover grill. Cook 15 to 20 minutes or until meat is done, rotating packs once during cooking.

Set foil packs on hot coals and cook 20 to 25 minutes or until meat is done, rotating packs partway through cooking time.

FOIL PACKS

FAN-FAVORITE SHRIMP PACKS

🏈 SERVES 4 🏈

- ✗ 1 (13.5 oz.) pkg. Andouille sausage
- ✗ 3 ears frozen or shucked fresh sweet corn
- ✗ 16 asparagus spears
- ✗ 1 lb. large peeled, cooked shrimp, tails removed
- ✗ 1 (8 oz.) pkg. sliced fresh mushrooms
- ✗ 1 or 2 lemons, sliced
- ✗ ¼ C. olive oil
- ✗ ¼ C. butter, sliced
- ✗ Salt, black pepper, and Old Bay seasoning to taste

Cut the sausage and corn into chunks and trim the ends off the asparagus spears.

Divide the cut-up food equally among four 18 x 24" sheets of heavy-duty foil that have been spritzed with cooking spray; add equal amounts of shrimp and mushrooms. Lay the lemon slices on top of the food. Drizzle each pack with 1 tablespoon oil; put pats of butter on top and sprinkle with salt, black pepper, and a generous amount of Old Bay. Double fold the tops and ends of the foil, sealing in the food and leaving some room inside for air to circulate.

Grill the packs over medium heat with the lid closed about 15 minutes, until the veggies are crisp-tender and shrimp are opaque, turning the packs once or twice. Open carefully to release steam away from your face.

HUDDLE UP!

In combo packs like these, cut the vegetables so they'll all finish cooking in the same amount of time.

TILAPIA & VEGGIES

🏈 SERVES 4 🏈

✗ 4 tilapia fillets, thawed if frozen
✗ ¼ C. mayonnaise
✗ ¼ C. grated Parmesan cheese
✗ Salt, paprika, cayenne & black pepper to taste

✗ 1 zucchini, sliced
✗ 2 carrots, peeled & cut into matchsticks
✗ ½ red bell pepper, thinly sliced
✗ 1 (12 oz.) pkg. frozen snap peas, partially thawed

Place each fillet on a large piece of sprayed foil; spread mayonnaise evenly over fillets. Sprinkle with cheese and all seasonings. Arrange zucchini, carrots, bell pepper, and snap peas over and around fish. Wrap foil around food to make four tent packs. Cook as directed.

COOKING METHODS

 Set foil packs on the grate over medium-high heat and cover grill. Cook 10 to 15 minutes or until fish flakes easily with a fork and vegetables are crisp-tender.

 Set foil packs on a few hot coals surrounded by more heat. Cook 10 to 15 minutes, rotating packs partway through cooking time, until fish flakes easily with a fork and vegetables are crisp-tender.

TAILGATE TRIVIA

Around 30–35% of tailgaters enjoy the party so much that they don't even attend the game!

FOIL PACKS

SALMON PITAS

🏈 MAKES 6 PITAS 🏈

- ✗ 1 (6 oz.) carton plain Greek yogurt
- ✗ 1 T. snipped fresh basil
- ✗ ¾ to 1 tsp. dried dill weed
- ✗ 4 (4 oz.) frozen salmon fillets, thawed
- ✗ 1 small red or yellow onion, thinly sliced
- ✗ 1 T. olive oil, divided
- ✗ Salt & pepper to taste
- ✗ 4 thin lemon slices, divided
- ✗ 6 pita bread pockets
- ✗ Chopped romaine lettuce
- ✗ 1 C. halved grape tomatoes

In a small bowl, mix yogurt, basil, and dill weed; cover and chill until serving time.

Pat fillets dry with paper towels. Place half the onion in the center of a large piece of sprayed foil and arrange two salmon pieces on top. Drizzle with 1½ teaspoons oil and sprinkle with salt and pepper. Top with two lemon slices and wrap foil around food in a tent pack. Repeat to make a second foil pack. Stack pita pockets together and wrap tightly in another piece of foil. Cook as directed.

ASSEMBLE & SERVE

Open the salmon packs and discard lemon slices. With a fork, pull salmon apart in chunks. Place some lettuce, salmon with onion, and tomatoes in each warm pita and serve with the chilled yogurt mixture.

COOKING METHODS

 Set salmon foil packs on the grate over medium-high heat and cover grill. Cook 10 to 12 minutes or until fish begins to flake with a fork. Warm the pita foil pack on the grate during the last 5 minutes of cooking time, turning once.

 Set salmon foil packs on a few hot coals and cook 10 to 12 minutes or until fish begins to flake with a fork. Heat the pita foil pack on warm coals during the last 5 minutes of cooking time, turning once.

SHRIMP TACOS

🏈 MAKES 8 TACOS 🏈

- ✗ 5 C. shredded cabbage
- ✗ 5 T. mayonnaise
- ✗ 1½ T. minced onion
- ✗ Zest & juice of 1 lime
- ✗ 1 lb. frozen raw shrimp, thawed & peeled

- ✗ ¼ C. butter, melted
- ✗ 2½ to 3 tsp. jerk seasoning (*recipe on page 127 or purchased*)
- ✗ Pinch of red pepper flakes
- ✗ Salt to taste

- ✗ Chopped fresh parsley
- ✗ 8 corn tortillas
- ✗ Fresh cilantro

In a bowl, stir together cabbage, mayonnaise, onion, and lime zest and juice. Cover and chill until needed.

Place shrimp in another bowl with butter, all seasonings, and some parsley; toss until evenly coated. Divide shrimp between two large pieces of doubled, sprayed foil and wrap to make two tent packs. Wrap tortillas in another piece of foil. Cook as directed and serve cabbage mixture and shrimp in the warm tortillas; garnish with cilantro.

COOKING METHODS

 Set shrimp foil packs on the grate over medium-high heat and cover grill. Cook 8 to 10 minutes or until shrimp are pink and fully cooked. Set tortilla foil pack over indirect medium heat until warm, about 5 minutes.

 Set shrimp foil packs on medium coals and cook 8 to 10 minutes or until shrimp are pink and fully cooked. Rotate packs and flip over halfway through cooking time. Set tortilla foil pack next to coals until warm.

JERK SEASONING

Mix 1 tablespoon dried minced onion, 1¼ teaspoons dried thyme, 1 teaspoon each ground allspice, garlic powder, and pepper, ½ teaspoon each cayenne pepper and paprika, and ¼ teaspoon each ground cinnamon and salt. Store in an airtight container and use the amount needed in recipes.

HUDDLE UP!

For convenience, prep the meat mixture ahead of time and refrigerate it in an airtight container until ready to use. Many foil packs can be prepped, assembled, and chilled until needed.

CHEESY STUFFED PEPPERS

🏈 **SERVES 4** 🏈

- ✗ 2 T. butter
- ✗ 2 T. olive oil
- ✗ 1 sweet onion, sliced in rings
- ✗ 6 oz. sliced baby bella mushrooms
- ✗ 1 T. minced garlic
- ✗ Salt & pepper to taste
- ✗ ½ lb. deli sliced roast beef
- ✗ 2 green bell peppers
- ✗ 8 slices provolone cheese, divided

In a skillet over medium heat, combine butter and oil; when hot, add onion, mushrooms, garlic, salt, and pepper. Sauté over low heat until onions and mushrooms are soft and caramelized, about 20 minutes. Add the beef and cook 10 minutes more.

Slice bell peppers in half lengthwise; remove stems, seeds, and white ribs. Line each pepper "shell" with a slice of cheese. Fill each shell generously with the meat mixture and top with another slice of cheese. Line four large pieces of foil with parchment paper. Wrap parchment-lined foil snugly around each stuffed pepper to make four flat packs. Cook as directed.

COOKING METHODS

 Set foil packs on the grate over medium heat and cover grill. Cook 15 to 20 minutes or until peppers are tender and cheese is melted.

Set foil packs on hot coals and cook 15 to 20 minutes or until peppers are tender and cheese is melted. Rotate the packs once or twice during cooking.

HUDDLE UP!

A melon baller works well to scoop out the zucchini.

FOIL PACKS

ZUCCHINI PIZZA BOATS

SERVES 4

- ✗ 2 medium zucchini
- ✗ Olive oil
- ✗ ½ lb. ground turkey or sausage
- ✗ 1 tsp. dried oregano
- ✗ 1 tsp. dried basil
- ✗ Salt & pepper to taste
- ✗ 1½ C. cheese & garlic pasta sauce (*or other spaghetti sauce*)
- ✗ ¾ C. shredded mozzarella cheese

Cut each zucchini in half horizontally and scoop out the center to make "boats" about ½" thick. Brush edges with
oil and set aside.

In a saucepan, heat 1 tablespoon oil. Add turkey, herbs, and seasonings; brown meat until crumbly. Drain off excess fat and stir in sauce; cook until heated through. Divide the turkey mixture evenly among zucchini boats and sprinkle with cheese; press lightly. Wrap each boat in parchment paper-lined foil to make four tent packs. Cook as directed.

COOKING METHODS

Set foil packs on the grate over medium heat and cover grill. Cook about 15 minutes or until tender.

Set foil packs on a few hot coals surrounded by more heat. Cook 15 to 20 minutes or until tender. Rotate packs once during cooking.

BUFFALO CHICKEN BREAD

🏈 SERVES 4 🏈

Slice a loaf of Vienna bread in half crosswise and lengthwise. Mix 2 tablespoons buffalo wing sauce, ¼ cup blue cheese dressing, and ½ cup ranch dressing. Reserve ¼ cup sauce mixture; spread remainder on bread. Toss 1½ cups cooked chicken with reserved sauce and arrange evenly on bread. Top each piece with ¼ cup each shredded cheddar and Monterey Jack, 2 tablespoons shredded Parmesan, and 1 tablespoon crumbled blue cheese; press lightly. Wrap in parchment paper-lined foil to make four flat packs. Cook as directed until hot and melty.

COOKING METHODS

Set foil packs on the grate over indirect medium heat and cover grill. Cook 25 to 30 minutes, rotating once.

Set foil packs on warm coals surrounded by more heat. Cook 10 to 20 minutes, rotating once.

HUDDLE UP!

Heavy-duty foil that's 18" wide works well for packs like these.

MEATBALL DINNER

🏈 SERVES 3 TO 4 🏈

- ✗ 1 C. chopped onion
- ✗ 5 or 6 medium red potatoes, scrubbed & quartered
- ✗ 3 carrots, peeled & sliced in rounds
- ✗ 1 C. fresh sliced mushrooms
- ✗ 1 lb. lean ground beef
- ✗ 1 T. Worcestershire sauce
- ✗ 1 tsp. minced garlic
- ✗ ½ C. cooked rice
- ✗ Barbecue sauce
- ✗ ¼ C. butter, softened
- ✗ 2 to 3 tsp. fresh rosemary (or ¾ tsp. dried)
- ✗ Salt & pepper to taste

Line three or four large pieces of foil with parchment paper. Divide the onion, potatoes, carrots, and mushrooms evenly among foil pieces and set aside.

In a large bowl, combine beef, Worcestershire sauce, garlic, and cooked rice; mix well with your hands. Lightly shape the mixture into 10 to 12 (1½") meatballs. Place three or four meatballs on the vegetables in each pack and drizzle with 2 tablespoons barbecue sauce.

In a small bowl, mix the butter and rosemary; add a few dollops to each pack. Season with salt and pepper and wrap the packs tent-style. Cook as directed.

COOKING METHODS

 Set foil packs on the grate over indirect high heat and cover grill. Cook about 30 minutes or until meat is done and vegetables are tender.

 Set foil packs on a few hot coals surrounded by more heat. Cook about 30 minutes or until meat is done and vegetables are tender. Rotate packs several times during cooking and place several hot coals on top of each pack during the last 10 minutes.

FOIL PACKS

SOUTHWESTERN CHICKEN

🏈 SERVES 4 🏈

- ✗ 1 (15 oz.) can black beans, drained & rinsed
- ✗ 2 C. frozen whole kernel corn
- ✗ 1 (10 oz.) can diced tomatoes & green chiles, drained
- ✗ ½ tsp. ground cumin
- ✗ 4 boneless, skinless chicken breast halves
- ✗ ½ C. shredded Mexican cheese blend
- ✗ Salsa for serving

In a bowl, stir together beans, corn, tomatoes, and cumin. Place each piece of chicken in the center of a large piece of sprayed foil. Spoon about 1 cup bean mixture over the chicken in each pack, dividing it evenly. Wrap foil around food to make four tent packs and cook as directed. Serve with salsa.

TAILGATE TRIVIA

The NFL didn't require helmets for players until 1943. Apparently before then players would grow their hair long to try to protect their heads.

COOKING METHODS

Set foil packs on the grate over medium-high heat and cover grill. Cook 15 to 20 minutes or until chicken is done (*internal temperature should reach 165°F*). Open the packs and sprinkle with cheese. Reseal and let rest until cheese melts, about 2 minutes.

Set foil packs on hot coals and cook 15 to 20 minutes or until chicken is done (*internal temperature should reach 165°F*). Rotate packs partway through cooking time. Open the packs and sprinkle with cheese. Reseal and let rest until cheese melts, about 2 minutes.

RANCH CHICKEN & VEGGIES

🏈 SERVES 2 🏈

- ✗ 2 boneless, skinless chicken breast halves
- ✗ ¼ tsp. Montreal Chicken Seasoning, divided
- ✗ ¼ C. ranch salad dressing, divided
- ✗ 2 T. water
- ✗ 2 C. quartered small red potatoes
- ✗ 2 carrots, peeled & sliced into sticks
- ✗ 2 C. fresh green beans, trimmed
- ✗ 2 T. shredded Parmesan cheese, divided

Set each chicken breast half on a large piece of sprayed foil. Sprinkle each chicken piece with ⅛ teaspoon Montreal seasoning and drizzle with 1 tablespoon dressing. In a large bowl, mix remaining 2 tablespoons dressing with water. Add potatoes, carrots, and green beans; stir until well coated. Divide vegetables evenly among chicken pieces and pour any remaining liquid around the edges. Sprinkle each with 1 tablespoon cheese. Wrap foil around food to make two tent packs and cook as directed.

COOKING METHODS

Set foil packs on the grate over medium heat and cover grill. Cook 20 to 25 minutes or until vegetables are crisp-tender and chicken is done (*internal temperature should reach 165°F*).

Set foil packs on medium coals and cook 25 to 30 minutes or until vegetables are crisp-tender and chicken is done (*internal temperature should reach 165°F*).

TAILGATE TIP

Some basics could make the difference for your party: take along toilet paper, plastic trash bags, rain gear, a first aid kit, sunscreen, and extra ice just in case.

HUDDLE UP!

Check meat several times to be sure packs retain moisture. Add water or more ice cubes, if necessary.

BBQ SHORT RIBS

🏈 SERVES 4 TO 6 🏈

✗ 2 lbs. boneless beef short ribs
✗ Dry rub seasoning (*recipe below or purchased*)
✗ 8 ice cubes
✗ Barbecue sauce

Generously coat the ribs with dry rub seasoning and place in a covered dish. Chill about 1 hour.

To cook, grease four double thicknesses of foil. Arrange two or three ribs on each foil piece along with two ice cubes. Wrap foil around meat to make four tent packs. Cook as directed and serve with barbeque sauce.

DRY RUB SEASONING

Stir together 1 tablespoon each brown sugar, paprika, and chili powder, 1 teaspoon each garlic powder and salt, and black pepper to taste. This makes enough dry rub to generously coat 2 to 3 lbs. of ribs or other cuts of beef.

COOKING METHODS

Set foil packs on the grate over indirect medium heat and cover grill. Cook 1½ to 2 hours or until tender. If desired, fold foil back and brush meat with barbeque sauce; cover grill and cook 5 minutes more.

Set foil packs on the grate over indirect medium heat and cover grill. Cook 1½ to 2 hours or until tender. If desired, fold foil back and brush meat with barbeque sauce; cover grill and cook 5 minutes more.

TAILGATE TRIVIA

In the 1880s, Walter Camp, a rugby player at Yale University, created the rules, positions, and scoring system for what became modern American football.

◀113

SIDES & SALADS

JUST CHILLIN' PASTA SALAD

🏈 SERVES A CROWD 🏈

Cook 1 lb. pasta (*I used shells, but any small shape will work*) to al dente, according to package directions; drain, rinse with cold water, and set aside to cool. Meanwhile, chop up ½ red onion, 1 green bell pepper, and 3 celery ribs and toss them into a big bowl. Cut 4 oz. cheddar cheese into small cubes and add to the bowl along with ½ to 1 (5 oz.) pkg. mini pepperoni.

In a small bowl, whisk together ½ cup creamy Italian dressing, 2 tablespoons mayo, and enough dried basil, salt, and black pepper to make your taste buds happy; add to the cooled pasta and stir to blend. Serve immediately or chill first (*if chilled, add a little more Italian dressing at serving time if it seems dry*).

TAILGATE SPINACH SALAD

Cook 1 cup orzo pasta according to package directions. In the meantime, in a big bowl, whisk together 3 tablespoons olive oil, 3 tablespoons red wine vinegar, 1 teaspoon Italian or Mediterranean seasoning blend, and salt and black pepper to taste.

Drain the pasta and rinse with cold water; add to the bowl and stir to coat. Gently stir in 4 cups lightly packed baby spinach (*coarsely chopped*), ¼ cup chopped dried tomatoes (*packed in oil*), and about 12 pitted Kalamata olives (*sliced*).

HUDDLE UP!

This is a tangy pasta salad with a distinctive Mediterranean vibe—and no mayo in sight! Perfect for any game-day appetite.

HOMETOWN CORN SALAD

🏈 MAKES ABOUT 7 CUPS 🏈

Remove the husks and silk from 6 ears of sweet corn. Brush the corn lightly with vegetable oil. Grill over medium heat until tender and lightly charred, turning occasionally. Set aside until just cool enough to handle.

Cut the kernels off the cobs and put the corn into a bowl. Core, seed, and dice a green bell pepper, ½ of a small red onion, and a couple of juicy Roma tomatoes and toss them in there, too (*you can also char the bell pepper before dicing it, if you'd like*); add a handful of chopped fresh cilantro, a big drizzle of olive oil, and a squeeze of fresh lime juice.

Season liberally with salt and black pepper and stir to combine. Chill at least 30 minutes for flavors to blend, and you'll be rewarded with crisp and smoky lusciousness!

TAILGATE TRIVIA

Green Bay Packers fans have braved the coldest weather while tailgating and supporting their team. During a 1967 game against the Cowboys (now known as the Ice Bowl), the wind chill was -48° F!

HUDDLE UP!

Pack salads and other side dishes into square containers with lids. They stack perfectly in your cooler, they're easy to grab at chow time, and if by chance there are any leftovers, just stack them back in your cooler.

FRUIT SALAD

🏈 MAKES ABOUT 12 CUPS 🏈

- ✗ 2 C. chopped fresh strawberries
- ✗ 2 (15 oz.) cans mandarin oranges, drained
- ✗ 2 C. chopped fresh apricots or peaches
- ✗ 2 C. green grapes
- ✗ 2 C. red grapes
- ✗ ¼ C. honey
- ✗ Zest and juice of 1 lime
- ✗ 2 C. fresh blackberries or blueberries

In a big bowl, combine the strawberries, mandarin oranges, apricots, and all the grapes. In a small bowl, whisk together the honey, lime zest, and lime juice. Chill until serving time.

When you're ready to eat, add the blackberries and the honey mixture to the big bowl of fruit; stir gently until coated.

POTATO SALAD

🏈 SERVES 8 TO 10 🏈

- ✗ 3 eggs
- ✗ 3 lbs. red-skinned potatoes
- ✗ Salt
- ✗ 8 dill pickle spears, diced
- ✗ 3 celery ribs, sliced
- ✗ ½ medium red onion, chopped
- ✗ ⅔ C. mayo
- ✗ 2 T. stone-ground mustard
- ✗ 2½ T. apple cider vinegar
- ✗ 2 T. chopped fresh dill weed
- ✗ Black pepper

Put the eggs in a single layer in a saucepan and add water to cover by 1". Bring to a boil; cover, remove from heat, and let stand 15 minutes. Drain, then fill the saucepan with cold water and ice; let stand until the eggs are cool. Peel under cold running water and set aside.

In the meantime, in a big saucepan, cook the potatoes in salted boiling water until just tender; drain and cool. Cut the potatoes into bite-size pieces and dump into a big bowl along with the pickles, celery, and onion.

In a small bowl, stir together the mayo, mustard, vinegar, and dill; pour the mixture over the vegetables in the bowl. Dice the cooled eggs and add to the bowl. Season with salt and black pepper and mix gently until blended.

HUDDLE UP!

Potato salad is an all-time favorite. Keep it well chilled until serving time, then return it to the cooler within 2 hours (*sooner if it's hot outside*).

POTATO SALAD ONIONS

🏈 **SERVES 4** 🏈

Preheat the grill on medium heat, for indirect cooking. Peel 4 medium yellow onions and cut off the top third of each, keeping the tops; trim the bottoms so they set flat. Dig out the center of each onion, leaving the two outer rings and the bottom intact. Save the portion you dug out for another recipe.

Stir together 1 cup prepared potato salad, ½ cup shredded cheddar cheese, and 4 cooked and crumbled bacon strips; spoon this mixture into the onion bowls and replace the tops. Wrap a piece of heavy-duty foil around each, leaving room inside for air circulation.

Grill on the cool side of the grill for 20 minutes, until tender. Open packet carefully to avoid steam.

GRILLED CAESAR

🏈 SERVES 6 🏈

- ✗ 1 clove garlic
- ✗ Salt
- ✗ 1 T. lemon juice
- ✗ 1 T. mayonnaise
- ✗ 1 tsp. anchovy paste

- ✗ 1 tsp. Dijon mustard
- ✗ 1 tsp. each Worcestershire sauce & Tabasco sauce
- ✗ 1 tsp. distilled white vinegar
- ✗ ¼ C. grated Parmesan cheese

- ✗ ¼ C. olive oil, plus more for brushing
- ✗ Black pepper to taste
- ✗ 3 Romaine lettuce hearts
- ✗ Shredded Parmesan cheese

In a bowl, mash together the garlic and ⅛ teaspoon salt to form a paste. Stir in the lemon juice, mayonnaise, anchovy paste, mustard, Worcestershire sauce, Tabasco sauce, vinegar, and the grated Parmesan. Add the oil in a slow, steady stream while whisking rapidly. Season with pepper and chill until serving time.

Preheat the grill and a grill pan on high heat. Cut the Romaine hearts in half lengthwise, brush with oil, and sprinkle with a little salt and pepper. Set the Romaine halves on the hot pan and grill until nicely charred and wilted, turning occasionally. Serve with the chilled dressing and top with some shredded Parmesan.

SUMMER VEGGIE SALAD

🏈 SERVES 4 🏈

- ✗ 1 zucchini
- ✗ 1 yellow summer squash
- ✗ 2 T. olive oil
- ✗ 1 T. lemon juice
- ✗ 1½ tsp. minced garlic
- ✗ 1 ear sweet corn, husks & silk removed
- ✗ ½ C. sunflower nuts
- ✗ 2 large carrots, peeled & shredded
- ✗ ½ (5 oz.) pkg. baby arugula
- ✗ 1 small red onion, peeled & sliced
- ✗ Parmesan cheese, sliced & cut into bite-size pieces
- ✗ Fresh basil & parsley, chopped
- ✗ Your favorite vinaigrette
- ✗ Skewers*

Using a mandolin slicer or a large vegetable peeler, make long slices (*ribbons*) of zucchini and squash. Place ribbons in a zippered plastic bag with the oil, lemon juice, and garlic; toss carefully to coat.

Grease the grill rack and preheat the grill on medium heat. Remove the ribbons from the bag and thread onto skewers. Coat the corn with cooking spray. Dump the nuts into a small foil pan. Set the pan, skewers, and corn on the grill rack. Heat the nuts until toasted, shaking the pan occasionally. Cook the ribbons for several minutes on each side, until grill marks appear. Cook the corn until tender and lightly charred; cut the kernels off the ear and place in a bowl with the ribbons and nuts. Set aside to cool.

Add the carrots, arugula, onion, and Parmesan to the bowl with the cooled veggies and toss in a little basil and parsley. Serve with the vinaigrette.

*Soak wooden skewers in water for ½ hour or use metal skewers.

SMOKIN' GRILLER BOURBON BEANS

Preheat a grill on low heat. Put 1 (11 x 15 x 3") foil pan inside another one and coat with cooking spray.

Drain 2 (3 lb. 5 oz.) cans pork and beans, 2 (15 oz.) cans black beans, 1 (15 oz.) can kidney beans, and 1 (15 oz.) can cannellini beans and dump into the pan. Add 1 (18 oz.) bottle BBQ sauce, 1 finely chopped jalapeño pepper, 1 chopped red onion, and 1 each chopped yellow and red bell pepper. Stir in 1 lb. chopped and cooked smoky bacon, up to 2 lbs. brown sugar (*go on—throw it in there*), and 1 cup bourbon.

Cover tightly with foil and place on the grill; close the grill lid and cook for ½ hour, until bubbly; remove the foil and cook ½ hour longer, until hot and awesome.

GRILLED VEGGIES IN A SNAP

🏈 SERVES 6 🏈

Preheat the grill on medium heat. Prepare fresh veggies by slicing into evenly sized pieces as needed (*I chopped up 16 cups of veggies, using a combination of red, green, yellow, and orange bell peppers, red onion, broccoli, mushrooms, and zucchini; I also used whole cherry tomatoes*). Toss them into a big bowl and add ½ cup vegetable oil, 3 tablespoons minced garlic, and salt, black pepper, and red pepper flakes to taste. Stir it all together, and dump onto a big grill pan, and set on the grill.

Close the grill lid and cook 10 to 15 minutes or until the veggies are crisp-tender and just starting to brown on the edges, stirring occasionally for even cooking.

TAILGATE TRIVIA

The University of Pennsylvania's Franklin Field is recognized by the NCAA as the oldest college football stadium. It is also believed to have hosted the most football games by any one college team.

SEASONED ROOT VEGETABLES

🏈 **SERVES 6** 🏈

- ✗ 2 T. apple cider vinegar
- ✗ ⅓ C. apple cider
- ✗ 2 T. olive oil
- ✗ 3 T. melted butter
- ✗ 2 T. chopped fresh rosemary
- ✗ Salt & black pepper to taste
- ✗ 2 turnips, peeled
- ✗ 1 lb. fingerling potatoes
- ✗ 3 medium kohlrabi, peeled
- ✗ 2 carrots, peeled
- ✗ 2 parsnips, peeled
- ✗ 1 red onion, peeled

In a big microwave-safe bowl, stir together the vinegar, apple cider, oil, butter, rosemary, salt, and pepper.

Cut the turnips, potatoes, kohlrabi, carrots, parsnips, and onion into even-size pieces and add to the cider mixture; stir to coat. Cover the bowl with microwave-safe plastic wrap and microwave on high for 10 minutes.

Preheat the grill on medium heat, for indirect cooking. Dump the vegetable mixture in a single layer in a 9 x 13" foil pan and set the pan on the cool side of the grill. Close the lid and cook for 45 minutes or until the vegetables are tender, stirring occasionally.

VEGGIE KABOBS

🏈 SERVES 6 🏈

- ✗ 1 each red & green bell pepper
- ✗ 1 zucchini
- ✗ 1 yellow summer squash
- ✗ 1 red onion
- ✗ 12 small whole mushrooms
- ✗ 12 cherry tomatoes
- ✗ ⅓ C. olive oil
- ✗ 3½ T. red wine vinegar
- ✗ 2 T. grated Romano cheese
- ✗ 1 tsp. sugar
- ✗ 1 tsp. coarse black pepper
- ✗ ¾ tsp. salt
- ✗ ¼ tsp. garlic powder
- ✗ Skewers*

Cut the bell peppers, zucchini, squash, and onion into big chunks and toss into a zippered plastic bag or a bowl; add the mushrooms and tomatoes.

In a jar with a tight-fitting lid, combine the oil, vinegar, Romano, sugar, pepper, salt, and garlic powder. Attach the lid, shake the jar like crazy, and pour the mixture into the bag with the vegetables; turn to coat. Chill for 1 hour, turning the bag occasionally.

Grease the grill rack and preheat the grill on medium-high heat. Remove the vegetables from the marinade and thread the pieces onto skewers; set the marinade aside.

Set skewers on the hot grill rack and cook for 10 minutes on each side or until grill marks appear and vegetables are tender, basting occasionally with the set-aside marinade.

Soak wooden skewers in water for ½ hour or use metal skewers.

TEAM VEGGIES

GARLIC & ONION ASPARAGUS

Mix 1 tablespoon olive oil and ½ teaspoon each garlic salt and onion powder in a foil pan. Add 1 lb. trimmed asparagus, turning to coat; arrange in a single layer. Top with several pats of butter, and set the pan on the hot grill for 6 to 8 minutes or until crisp-tender. Toss and serve.

SIMPLY CARROTS

Preheat the grill on medium-high heat. Place 1 lb. small carrots (*or cut larger ones in half lengthwise*) on parchment paper-lined heavy-duty foil, drizzle with 2 teaspoons grape-seed oil, and season well with salt and black pepper. Fold up the foil, leaving room inside for air circulation, and set on the hot grill for 15 minutes or until crisp-tender. Open carefully, toss, and serve.

CAULIFLOWER WITH PARMESAN

Preheat the grill on medium heat. Break 1 head cauliflower into florets and put into a bowl. Add ¼ cup melted butter, 1½ teaspoons seasoned salt, and ¼ cup Parmesan cheese; toss to coat. Dump the mixture onto a big piece of heavy-duty foil. Fold up the foil, leaving room inside for air circulation, and set on the hot grill. Cook for 10 to 15 minutes or until crisp-tender. Open carefully, toss, and serve.

ITALIAN SNAP PEAS

Preheat the grill on medium heat. Line the grill rack with heavy-duty foil and arrange 1 lb. snap peas on the foil; toss on 1 sliced green onion. Drizzle with 1½ tablespoons melted butter and sprinkle with 1½ teaspoons chopped fresh oregano, 1½ teaspoons lemon zest, ¾ teaspoon salt, and ½ teaspoon black pepper. Cook about 8 minutes or until crisp-tender. Toss and serve.

SIDES & SALADS

CHIPOTLE-LIME CAULIFLOWER STEAKS

🏈 SERVES 8 🏈

- ✗ **2 large heads cauliflower, leaves removed**
- ✗ **Zest & juice of 2 limes, divided**
- ✗ **2 T. paprika**
- ✗ **1 T. chipotle seasoning (like Mrs. Dash Southwest Chipotle)**
- ✗ **1 tsp. coarse salt**
- ✗ **¼ C. olive oil or grape-seed oil**
- ✗ **1 tsp. finely minced garlic**
- ✗ **1 tsp. agave nectar**
- ✗ **¼ c. fresh cilantro**

Grease the grill rack and preheat the grill on high heat. Using a sharp knife, trim off just enough of the cauliflower stems so the heads set flat. Then, starting at the top of each head, cut 1"-thick slices (*steaks*).

In a small bowl, mix the lime zest, paprika, chipotle seasoning, and salt. In a separate small bowl, whisk together the oil and lime juice. Whisk in the garlic and agave nectar.

Brush one side of each cauliflower steak with the oil mixture and sprinkle generously with the seasoning mixture. Set the steaks on the hot grill rack, seasoned side down. Oil and season the top side. Close the lid and cook for 5 minutes; flip the steaks, cover, and cook 5 minutes longer or until crisp-tender. To serve, scatter cilantro over the top.

BREAKAWAY BUTTERS

BACON-BLUE CHEESE BUTTER

Bacon-Blue Cheese Mix ½ cup softened butter with 1 tablespoon finely chopped cooked bacon and 1½ tablespoons crumbled blue cheese.

CHILI BUTTER

Chili Mix ½ cup softened butter with 2 teaspoons Worcestershire sauce, ½ teaspoon hot sauce, and 2 teaspoons each chili powder & dried oregano. Stir in ½ teaspoon each ground cumin, paprika, garlic powder & onion powder.

HUDDLE UP!

Refrigerate all butters 1 to 2 hours to blend flavors; bring to room temperature before serving.

CILANTRO-LIME BUTTER

Cilantro-Lime Mix ½ cup softened butter with 2 tablespoons chopped fresh cilantro, the zest and juice of ½ lime, 1 teaspoon salt, and ½ teaspoon cayenne pepper.

GARLIC HERB BUTTER

Garlic, Herb & Parm Mix ½ cup softened butter with 2 teaspoons minced garlic, ¼ C. grated Parmesan cheese, and 2 tablespoons each fresh chopped parsley, basil & green onion. Season with salt and black pepper.

HORSERADISH BUTTER

Horseradish Mix ½ cup softened butter with ⅓ cup chopped fresh chives, 3 tablespoons prepared horseradish, 1 teaspoon salt, and ½ teaspoon lemon zest.

CHEESY RED POTATOES

🏈 **SERVES 8** 🏈

- ✗ 16 baby red potatoes
- ✗ ¼ C. olive oil
- ✗ 1 tsp. each garlic powder, salt & black pepper
- ✗ ½ lb. farmer's cheese, cut into 16 (2") squares, about ¼" thick
- ✗ 2 T. chopped fresh chives
- ✗ Skewers*

Place potatoes in a big microwave-safe bowl with ¼ cup water. Microwave uncovered on high power for 10 minutes or until just tender; drain and set aside until cool enough to handle. Slice off one end of each potato to create a flat top.

In a big bowl, mix oil, garlic powder, salt, and pepper. Add potatoes and toss to coat. Cover and chill for 1 hour.

Grease the grill rack and preheat the grill on medium heat. Thread the chilled potatoes onto the skewers with all flat tops facing the same direction; set them on the grill rack, flat sides down. Close the grill lid and cook about 5 minutes, until grill marks appear. Flip so flat tops face up and set a cheese square on each flat surface. Close the lid until the cheese melts. Sprinkle immediately with chives and pepper.

Serve with sour cream, if you'd like.

*Soak wooden skewers in water for ½ hour or use metal skewers.

SWEET POTATOES WITH A KICK

🏈 SERVES 4 🏈

- ✗ 3 large sweet potatoes
- ✗ Zest & juice of 1 large lime
- ✗ Pinch of cayenne pepper
- ✗ 1 T. coarse salt
- ✗ Canola oil
- ✗ Coarse black pepper to taste
- ✗ ¼ C. chopped fresh cilantro

Pierce the sweet potatoes several times and microwave on high for 4 minutes or until barely tender; cool until easy to handle. Mix the lime zest, cayenne, and salt; set aside.

Grease the grill rack and preheat the grill on medium heat. Cut each partially cooked sweet potato into 1"-thick wedges; brush with oil and season with a little pepper. Put the wedges on the hot grill rack and cook several minutes on each side, until grill marks appear and sweet potatoes are tender.

Remove the wedges from the grill and brush with a little more oil; sprinkle with the set-aside lime zest mixture, toss on the cilantro, and drizzle with lime juice.

FULLBACK POTATO BAR

🏈 SERVES 8 🏈

GRILL-BAKED POTATOES

Poke holes in 8 baking potatoes; wrap in foil. Cook over indirect heat 45 minutes, until tender.

SLICED POTATOES

Cut 5 lbs. of potatoes into ½"-thick slices; put into a bowl with 1 cup chopped onions, ¼ cup chopped shallots, 3 tablespoons olive oil, 2 tablespoons seasoned salt, 1 teaspoon garlic salt, and some black pepper. Dump into a greased 9 x 13" foil pan, cover with foil, and set over direct low heat for 30 minutes, until tender.

POTATO TOTS

Put a big handful of thawed tots on eight squares of greased foil; season to taste. Fold foil around tots and heat over direct low heat 15 minutes.

START HERE FOR INSPIRATION

The Basics
Butter
Sour cream
Shredded cheese

Fantastic Finishes
Fresh basil, cilantro, dill & chives
Seasoned salt, garlic salt & onion salt
Crushed red pepper

Tantalizing Toppers
Cooked bacon, ham & turkey
Pepperoni slices
Veggies like broccoli & asparagus

Grilled corn kernels
Green onions
Tomatoes
Mushrooms
Guacamole

Cheese sauce
Chili
Gravy
Pesto
Salsa

SET IT UP

Load the grill with potatoes. While the potatoes cook, set the table with plates, silverware, napkins, and glasses. Put your favorite wines on ice. Place toppings in bowls. Add the potatoes to the table when they're cooked.

LOADED CHEESE FRIES

🏈 SERVES 4 TO 6 🏈

Chop and cook ½ lb. bacon, reserving 1 tablespoon grease from the pan. In the meantime, preheat the grill on medium heat.

Dump a 2 lb. bag of frozen crinkle-cut fries into a greased 9 x 13" foil pan. Sprinkle evenly with 12 oz. shredded sharp cheddar cheese. Top with 4 oz. cream cheese (*cubed*), 4 sliced green onions, and the cooked bacon. In a bowl, stir together the reserved bacon grease, 2 tablespoons olive oil, 2 large cloves garlic (*finely chopped*), ½ teaspoon red pepper flakes, and salt and black pepper to taste; drizzle evenly over the fries.

Cover with greased foil and set on the grill about 30 minutes or until everything is sizzling hot, the fries are tender, and the cheese is melted.

TAILGATE TRIVIA

Tailgating might not have taken off without the 1866 invention of the chuckwagon by Charles Goodnight.

FIRECRACKER WATERMELON

🏈 SERVINGS VARY 🏈

Grease the grill rack and preheat the grill on medium-high heat. In the meantime, cut 1 mini watermelon into 1"-thick slices; cut each slice into four even pieces and sprinkle with salt and black pepper. Set the melon on the hot grill rack and cook for a few minutes on each side until grill marks appear; set aside to cool slightly.

At serving time, drizzle the slices with lime juice and honey. Top with jalapeño slices, crumbled feta cheese, and fresh cilantro.

TAILGATE TRIVIA

The huddle was started by Paul D. Hubbard, a deaf quarterback playing in the 1890s who didn't want the other teams to read his hand signals.

PULL-APART BREAD

🏈 SERVES A CROWD 🏈

- ✗ 1 (1 lb.) round loaf rye bread
- ✗ 8 oz. shredded dill
- ✗ Havarti cheese
- ✗ ½ lb. dried beef (*aka smoked beef*), chopped
- ✗ ½ C. unsalted butter, melted
- ✗ 1 to 2 T. dry ranch dressing mix
- ✗ Dill weed to taste

Preheat the grill on medium-low heat for indirect cooking. Cut the bread from the top down in ¾"-wide lengthwise and crosswise slices, without cutting through the bottom; set on a large sheet of heavy-duty foil and roll the foil up around the sides of the bread, creating a nest to hold the bread in place.

Set aside ¼ of the cheese and push the remainder into the cuts of the bread along with all the beef. Stir together the butter and ranch dressing mix and drizzle evenly over the top. Sprinkle the set-aside cheese and the dill weed over all. Cover with a piece of foil and place the loaf on the cool side of the grill. Close the lid and cook 12 to 15 minutes, rotating once or twice.

Remove the top piece of foil, close the lid again, and cook 12 to 15 minutes longer, rotating occasionally.

REVVIN' BEER BREAD

🏈 MAKES 1 LOAF 🏈

Preheat the oven to 375°F and grease a 5 x 9" loaf pan. In a mixing bowl, combine 3 cups flour, 1 tablespoon baking powder, 1 teaspoon salt, and 2 tablespoons sugar; beat in 1 egg until well mixed. Pour in 1 cup of beer (*that cheap pale ale that's hiding in your fridge is just fine*) and mix until the dough becomes sticky and forms a ball; set aside.

In a separate bowl, beat together 8 oz. cream cheese (*softened*), ½ teaspoon onion powder, 1 teaspoon garlic salt, ½ to 1 cup diced jalapeños (*fresh or pickled*), and 1 cup shredded cheddar cheese; fold into the set-aside dough until just mixed. Put the dough into the prepped loaf pan and top with a little more shredded cheddar and some more jalapeño slices.

Bake 50 to 60 minutes, until nice and brown. Cool for a bit before removing from the pan. Cool completely before slicing.

UNIFORM CORNBREAD SLABS

🏈 SERVINGS VARY 🏈

Make an 8.5 oz. pkg. of corn muffin mix according to package directions and bake in an 8 x 8" pan (*or whip up a batch using your favorite recipe*). Let cool, then cut into squares (*if more than ¾" thick, slice in half horizontally, too*). Beat together ½ cup softened butter, 1 finely diced jalapeño, and 2 tablespoons honey.

   Preheat the grill on medium-high heat. Coat the cornbread slices with cooking spray and set on the grill for a couple of minutes on each side, until crispy. Spread the butter mixture on the cornbread and serve immediately.

DESSERTS

MARGARITA BARS

🏈 MAKES 18 🏈

- ✗ 1 C. butter, softened
- ✗ 1 C. coarsely crushed pretzels
- ✗ 3½ C. sugar, divided
- ✗ Flour
- ✗ 3 limes
- ✗ ½ C. tequila or lime juice
- ✗ 6 large eggs at room temperature
- ✗ ½ C. powdered sugar

Preheat the oven to 350°F. Mix the butter, pretzels, ½ cup of the sugar, and 1 cup plus 1 tablespoon flour until well combined. Spread evenly in the bottom and ¼" to ½" up the sides of a greased 9 x 13" baking pan. Bake 12 to 15 minutes or until light golden brown. Remove from the oven and set aside while you make the filling. Don't turn off the oven.

Zest the limes and then squeeze their juice into a 1-cup measuring cup until you have about ½ cup of juice; fill to the 1 cup mark with tequila and pour the mixture into a big bowl. Stir in the eggs, the remaining 3 cups sugar, 1 cup flour, and about ⅔ of the zest until well combined; pour the filling into the partially cooled crust. Bake for an additional 30 to 35 minutes or until the center is set. Set aside until cool. Meanwhile mix the remaining lime zest with the powdered sugar; set aside.

When the bars are cool, cut into serving-size pieces. Stir the powdered sugar mixture and sprinkle evenly over the bars.

WINNING SUGAR COOKIES

🏈 MAKES ABOUT 2 DOZEN 2½" COOKIES 🏈

Cream 1 cup unsalted butter (*softened*) in a mixing bowl, then gradually beat in ¾ cupsugar. Beat in 1 egg, 2 teaspoons vanilla, and ¼ teaspoon salt until well mixed. Stir in 2½ cups flour, a little at a time, until incorporated. Divide the dough in half, wrap in plastic, and chill overnight. Remove dough from fridge and let stand at room temperature until softened. Roll out on a floured surface to ¼" thickness and cut out as desired (*baseballs, footballs, race cars . . . the choice is yours*). Bake on cookie sheets lined with parchment paper at 350°F for 12 to 15 minutes, until the edges just start to turn brown; remove from the cookie sheets and cool.

Decorate as desired using your favorite frosting. Wait until set before packing into a container, with waxed paper between layers.

CAST IRON COOKIE

🏈 SERVES A CROWD 🏈

Preheat the grill on low heat. In a big bowl, mix 1 cup softened butter, 1 cup brown sugar, and 1 cup sugar until light and fluffy; beat in 2 eggs and 1 tablespoon vanilla. Slowly add 3 cups flour, ¾ teaspoon baking soda, 1 teaspoon sea salt, and ½ cup quick oats, mixing until blended. Stir in 1½ cups baking chips (*I used a combination of semi-sweet chocolate chunks, semisweet mini chips, and white chips*).

    Grease a 12" cast iron skillet with shortening and press the dough into it. Set on the grill, close the lid, and cook until golden brown and done in the middle, rotating the pan occasionally (*this could take 25 minutes or longer, depending on the heat of your grill—don't rush it*). Cool slightly before cutting.

COCONUT-LIME MACAROONS

🏈 MAKES ABOUT 38 🏈

Mix 1 (14 oz.) pkg. sweetened flaked coconut, the zest of 2 limes, and 1 (14 oz.) can sweetened condensed milk. Scoop compact 1 tablespoon mounds onto baking sheets lined with parchment paper and coated with cooking spray. Bake for 15 minutes or until golden brown.

TAILGATE TRIVIA

Three United States universities are close enough to lakes or rivers that fans can "sailgate" on boats: the University of Washington, the University of Tennessee, and Baylor University.

STRAWBERRY CHEESECAKE POPPERS

🏈 MAKE AS MANY AS YOU NEED 🏈

Scoop out the center of large ripe strawberries; trim their bottoms flat. Fill berries with ready-to-eat cheesecake filling; sprinkle with cinnamon graham cracker crumbs.

TAILGATE TRIVIA

The Miami Dolphins are the only NFL team to have a perfect undefeated season. In 1972, they didn't lose (or tie) a single game!

BROWN SUGAR CAKE

🏈 SERVES 12 TO 15 🏈

- ✗ ½ C. shortening
- ✗ ½ C. sugar
- ✗ ²¾ C. brown sugar, divided
- ✗ 1¼ C. butter, softened, divided
- ✗ 3 tsp. vanilla, divided
- ✗ 5 eggs
- ✗ 3 C. flour
- ✗ ½ tsp. baking powder
- ✗ ¼ tsp. salt
- ✗ 1¼ C. milk, divided
- ✗ 1¼ C. toasted, chopped pecans, divided
- ✗ 2 C. powdered sugar, sifted

Preheat the oven to 350°F. Spray a 10" tube pan with cooking spray; set aside. In a mixing bowl, beat the shortening, sugar, 2¼ cups brown sugar, 1 cup butter, and 2 teaspoons vanilla. Add the eggs, one at a time, beating well after each. In a separate bowl, mix the flour, baking powder, and salt; add to the butter mixture alternately with 1 cup of the milk, beating well. Stir in 1 cup of the pecans; spread in the prepped pan. Bake 1¼ hours or until a wooden skewer inserted in the center comes out clean, covering with foil during last 15 minutes to prevent overbrowning. Set on a cooling rack for 10 minutes, then remove the cake from the pan and set upright to cool.

Melt the remaining ¼ cup butter in a saucepan over medium-low heat. Add the remaining ½ cup brown sugar and cook 2 minutes, stirring constantly. Add the remaining ¼ cup milk and bring to a boil, stirring constantly. Remove from the heat and stir in the remaining 1 teaspoon vanilla. Whisk in the powdered sugar until smooth, and immediately spread over the cooled cake; quickly sprinkle with the remaining ¼ cup pecans, pressing to adhere. Slice and serve.

NUTTY BROWNIES

🏈 **MAKES 9** 🏈

- ✗ ½ C. plus 2 T. butter, softened
- ✗ 6 T. unsweetened cocoa powder
- ✗ A big handful of semi-sweet chocolate chips
- ✗ 1¼ C. sugar
- ✗ 1½ tsp. vanilla
- ✗ 3 eggs
- ✗ 1¼ C. flour
- ✗ ¼ tsp. salt
- ✗ ½ C. chopped mixed nuts

Preheat the oven to 350°F. Grease the bottom only of an 8" square baking pan.

In a saucepan over low heat, melt together ½ cup of the butter, cocoa powder, and chocolate chips, stirring occasionally. Remove from the heat and stir in the sugar and vanilla. Add eggs one at a time, stirring well after each addition. Stir in the flour and salt until well combined and smooth. Stir in the nuts.

Spread the mixture evenly in the prepped pan and bake 25 to 32 minutes, until the brownies just begin to pull away from the sides of the pan. Do not over-bake. Cool completely before cutting.

BANANA SPLIT STICKS

Servings Vary

Cut cooled brownies into bite-size squares. Push onto wooden skewers alternately with banana chunks, pineapple chunks, and strawberries. For extra yum, serve with marshmallow ice cream topping for dipping.

TROPHY-WORTHY DONUT SHORTCAKES

🏈 MAKES 8 🏈

Line the grill grate with foil and spritz with cooking spray. Preheat the grill on low heat. In a bowl, stir together ¼ cup sugar and 1 tablespoon cinnamon. In a separate bowl, mix ¼ cup melted butter with 2 tablespoons brown sugar. Set both aside. Separate the biscuits from a 16 oz. tube of jumbo refrigerated buttermilk biscuits; push a hole through the center of each.

Arrange the biscuits on the foil. Close the grill lid and cook 4 to 5 minutes on each side, until browned on the outside and cooked through. Remove the biscuits from the grill; one at a time, dip both sides in the butter mixture and toss around in the cinnamon-sugar to coat. Top with spray whipped cream and pile on the fresh fruit.

BERRIES & POUND CAKE

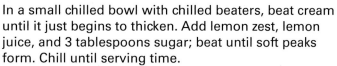

SERVES 6

- ✗ 1 C. whipping cream
- ✗ 1 tsp. lemon zest, plus more for sprinkling
- ✗ 1 T. lemon juice
- ✗ 5 T. sugar, divided
- ✗ 1½ C. cubed strawberries
- ✗ 1½ C. blueberries
- ✗ 1 T. chopped fresh mint
- ✗ 1 (10.75 oz.) pkg. frozen pound cake, thawed
- ✗ 2 T. softened butter

In a small chilled bowl with chilled beaters, beat cream until it just begins to thicken. Add lemon zest, lemon juice, and 3 tablespoons sugar; beat until soft peaks form. Chill until serving time.

Preheat the grill on medium heat. In an 8 x 8" foil pan, mix the strawberries, blueberries, mint, and remaining 2 tablespoons sugar. Close the lid and cook until the berries are hot and juicy, about 10 minutes, stirring occasionally.

Cut the cake into six slices and spread butter over both cut sides. Set the slices directly on the grill rack and cook a few minutes on each side until golden brown.

Serve berries over cake with the chilled whipped cream and sprinkle with more lemon zest.

CELEBRATION POUND CAKE

🏈 MAKES 16 🏈

Mix 8 oz. softened cream cheese, 3 tablespoons brown sugar, and ⅛ teaspoon cinnamon; set aside. Line the grill grate with foil, spritz with cooking spray, and preheat the grill on low heat. Core a fresh pineapple and cut into ½"-thick rings; sprinkle both sides with brown sugar and cinnamon and arrange rings on the foil. Cut 16 (*1" thick*) slices of pound cake (*I used plain and pumpkin-flavored*) and set on the foil. Heat everything until grill marks appear on both sides, flipping once.

Remove from the grill and spread the set-aside cream cheese mixture over the cake slices. Add a pineapple ring (*cut in half if needed*), caramel ice cream topping, and toasted chopped pecans.

TAILGATE TRIVIA

The longest field goal was 69 yards— kicked in 1976 by Ove Johansson of Abilene Christian University. That's three yards longer than the NFL record set by Justin Tucker in 2021.

BOOZY BANANA BOATS

🏈 SERVINGS VARY 🏈

Set a grill pan on the grill and preheat on high heat. For each banana, whisk together 1½ teaspoons honey, 1½ teaspoons rum, and a sprinkle of cinnamon. Cut unpeeled bananas lengthwise through the stem ends, following the curve of the fruit. Coat the grill pan and the cut side of each banana with cooking spray; set bananas on the hot pan, cut side down. Grill for a couple of minutes, until nice grill marks appear.

Flip them over and brush liberally with the honey-rum mixture before taking them off the grill. Spray on some whipping cream and dig in.

FRUIT TART

🏈 SERVES 6 🏈

- ✗ 2 T. cream cheese, softened
- ✗ 2 T. sugar, divided, plus more for sprinkling
- ✗ Flour
- ✗ 1 sheet frozen puff pastry, thawed according to package directions
- ✗ 1 or 2 peaches, pitted & sliced
- ✗ 2 or 3 apricots, pitted & sliced
- ✗ ⅔ C. blueberries
- ✗ Olive oil

Beat together the cream cheese and 1 tablespoon sugar until smooth; set aside. Crumple up aluminum foil to make several 2" to 3" diameter balls; set them on the grill rack and set a pizza stone on top of them. Preheat the grill on low to allow the stone to heat up slowly.

Line a cookie sheet with parchment paper; sprinkle with flour and unfold the pastry on top of it. With a knife, score the dough to form a 1" border around the outside edges. Sprinkle the border with 1 tablespoon sugar. Using a fork, pierce the dough several times inside the border. Increase the grill temperature to medium. Slide the dough, along with the parchment, onto the hot stone and cook for 15 minutes, until the dough is cooked through, rotating the pan as needed for even cooking.

Meanwhile, place the peaches and apricots in a foil pan, put the blueberries in a separate foil pan, and drizzle all the fruit with oil. Put pans on the grill and cook until slightly softened; set aside.

Gently spread the set-aside cream cheese mixture inside the border of the pastry and arrange cooked fruit on top. Sprinkle a little more sugar over the fruit, if you'd like.

GRILLED PINEAPPLE STICKS

🏈 MAKES 6 🏈

Peel and core a pineapple; cut into six wedges and put into a zippered plastic bag. Add 1 C. coconut milk, seal the bag, and chill overnight. Grease the grill rack and preheat the grill on medium heat; set the pineapple on the grill for several minutes on each side to get those coveted grill marks. Sprinkle with brown sugar and toasted coconut.

TAILGATE TRIVIA

Tailgating isn't just for sports fans—fans of Jimmy Buffet host huge tailgating parties before (and after) his concerts.

HUDDLE UP!

The cookies could be baked in the oven while the fruit is grilling, but I recommend using the grill to give them smokiness . . . and give you bragging rights.

FRUIT PIZZA

🏈 **SERVES 12** 🏈

- ✗ 1 (16.5 oz.) roll refrigerated chocolate chip cookie dough
- ✗ 1 lb. fresh strawberries, trimmed
- ✗ 2 or 3 kiwifruit, peeled
- ✗ Strawberry jam

Split the roll of dough in half; roll each half into a ¼"-thick circle on a greased piece of foil. Slide onto cookie sheets and refrigerate for an hour.

Preheat the grill on medium heat, for indirect cooking. Cut the strawberries in half lengthwise. Cut the kiwi into thick slices. Set aside.

Slide the cookie crusts, along with the foil, onto the cool side of the grill; close the lid and cook for 8 to 10 minutes or until golden brown and the edges are set. Remove the cookies from the grill and set aside (*the cookies will continue to cook while they set*).

Set a grill pan on the grill to preheat. Arrange the fruit on the hot pan and cook over direct heat until the fruit just begins to soften, then flip and heat briefly.

When you're ready to eat, spread jam over the crusts and arrange the grilled fruit on top. Slice and eat immediately.

PEANUT BUTTER POPCORN

🏈 MAKES ABOUT 12 CUPS 🏈

Dump 10 cups salted popcorn into a big bowl and line a big rimmed baking sheet with foil; set aside. Melt 3 tablespoons butter in a medium saucepan. Add 3 cups mini marshmallows, stirring until melted. Remove from the heat and stir in ½ cup creamy peanut butter.

Slowly pour the hot mixture over the popcorn, stirring until evenly coated. Transfer the coated popcorn to the prepped baking sheet and press 1 cup peanut butter M&Ms into the warm peanut butter (*add more if you'd like—there are no rules here*); set aside to cool. Break into pieces to serve.

HUDDLE UP!
Use packaged popped corn. Quick and delicious—and no hulls!

Honey Peaches

Spiced Apple Rings

Brown Sugar Pears

Zesty Blackberries

FRIENDLY RIVALS

HONEY PEACHES

Beat ½ cup heavy cream with 2 teaspoons honey until stiff peaks form; chill. Slice 3 peaches in half, remove the pits, and brush with honey. Grease the grill rack and preheat the grill on low heat. Grill the peaches for several minutes on each side, until grill marks appear. Serve with the chilled whipped cream. Top with fresh berries.

SPICED APPLE RINGS

In a bowl, mix ⅔ cup orange juice, 2 tablespoons honey, 1 tablespoon chopped fresh mint, 1 teaspoon vanilla, ½ teaspoon ground ginger, and ¼ teaspoon black pepper. Core 2 apples, cut into ¼"-thick rings, and add to the bowl; chill 2 hours. Grease the grill rack and preheat the grill on medium heat. Grill the apple rings for 3 minutes on each side or until grill marks appear, basting often with the juice remaining in the bowl.

BROWN SUGAR PEARS

Grease the grill rack and preheat the grill on medium heat. Cut 2 pears into four wedges each. In a small bowl, mix ¼ cup melted butter and 1 tablespoon vanilla. In another bowl, mix ½ cup brown sugar and ¾ teaspoon cinnamon. Dip pear wedges into the butter mixture and then the brown sugar mixture. Set wedges on grill, close the lid, and cook several minutes on each side until grill marks appear. Serve with ice cream.

ZESTY BLACKBERRIES

Preheat the grill on medium heat. Line the grill rack with a piece of heavy-duty foil. In a bowl, stir together 2 cups blackberries, 1 to 2 tablespoons sugar, and 1 teaspoon orange zest. Brush 1 tablespoon melted unsalted butter onto the foil; toss on the blackberries, close the lid, and cook for 3 minutes or until the berries are juicy and slightly softened, stirring once. Serve over ice cream with a little extra orange zest.

HUDDLE UP!
The toffee can be stored in an airtight container for several days.

SALTED CHOCO-NUT TOFFEE

🏈 SERVES A CROWD 🏈

Line a big rimmed baking sheet with parchment paper. Melt 1¼ cups unsalted butter in a big saucepan over medium heat. Stir in 1 cup sugar, ⅓ cup brown sugar, 1 tablespoon instant espresso powder, 1 tablespoon molasses, and ⅓ cup water. Boil until a candy thermometer reaches 300°F, stirring often (*be patient—it takes a while*).

Remove from the heat, stir in 2 cups chopped pecans, and spread evenly in the prepped baking sheet. Sprinkle 1½ cups dark chocolate chips evenly over the top. When the chocolate has softened, spread it over the toffee and sprinkle on a light dusting of coarse salt. Let stand until firm, then break into pieces.

TAILGATE TRIVIA

College footballs are different from professional footballs. They have white bands painted on both ends to make the ball easier to spot when it's passed between players.

BEVERAGES

ALCOHOL-BASED DRINKS

ALCOHOL-FREE DRINKS

ALCOHOL-BASED DRINKS

CITRUS BLAST MARGARITAS

🏈 MAKES ABOUT 3 CUPS 🏈

Cut 3 limes, 3 lemons, and 2 oranges in half; dip the cut sides in sugar. Set cut side down on a hot grill pan until lightly charred. Juice the grilled fruit into a pitcher, add any accumulated juice from the pan, and stir in 8 oz. tequila and 6 oz. simple syrup (or to taste); chill. Pour drinks into ice-filled glasses rimmed with sugar; add fresh fruit slices if you'd like. Tipsy fun around the grill!

TAILGATE TRIVIA

Tailgating at the annual Florida-Georgia game is serious party business that can last for days. The event is even known to some as the World's Largest Outdoor Cocktail Party.

TROPICAL PARTY PUNCH

🏈 MAKES ABOUT 20 SERVINGS 🏈

Ahead of time, chill a 1.75-liter bottle of coconut rum, a 1-liter bottle of blue curaçao, 64 oz. of pineapple juice (or more to taste), and 8 oz. sweet and sour mix. Pour everything together into a 6-qt. drink dispenser and fill with ice. Everybody needs a little "Vitamin C" now and then, right? Drink up!

BEVERAGES

ALCOHOL-BASED DRINKS

SPIKED ICED TEA

🏈 MAKES ABOUT 8½ CUPS 🏈

Mix the zest of 1 lemon with ¼ cup sugar; set aside. Cut the zested lemon in half and set one half aside. Squeeze the juice from the other half into a 3-qt. pitcher. Stir in 3 cups of prepared lemonade, 3 cups of sun tea or unsweetened iced tea, 1 cup of bourbon, and 1 cup of sugar; chill.

Rub the rims of drinking glasses with the set-aside lemon half and dip rims into the sugar mixture. Fill with ice and pour in the tea mixture. Sippin' sensational!

TAILGATE TIP

Use cardboard six-pack holders to organize your favorite spices, hot sauces, and other condiments.

ALCOHOL-BASED DRINKS

SIMPLE SUMMER BEER

🏈 **MAKES ABOUT 9 CUPS** 🏈

BEVERAGES

Pour 4 cans of your favorite light beer into a big pitcher. Add one 12-oz. can frozen limeade, lemonade, or pink lemonade concentrate (thawed); fill the now-empty concentrate can with vodka and pour it into the pitcher. Mix it up and pour into ice-filled glasses. Plunk in some lime slices (or lemon slices if you're using lemonade) and call it a day.

ALCOHOL-BASED DRINKS

PARTY TIME SANGRIA

🏈 MAKES 4 SERVINGS 🏈

In a medium bowl, combine one 3-oz. package of strawberry gelatin and one 3-oz. package of lemon gelatin. Add 1½ cups of boiling water, stirring for two minutes or until completely dissolved.

In a two-cup measuring cup, combine 1 cup of red wine with enough ice cubes to fill the measuring cup to 1½ cups. Add to the gelatin mixture, stirring until the ice melts and the gelatin is slightly thickened (or refrigerate 10 to 15 minutes to thicken slightly, removing any unmelted ice).

Slice 8 fresh strawberries and drain one 11-oz. can of mandarin oranges. Cut 1 cup of seedless red grapes in half, if desired. Divide fruit evenly between four 12- to 18-oz. clear glass dessert dishes or wine glasses.

Pour gelatin mixture evenly over fruit in glasses, stirring carefully to distribute fruit. Refrigerate 4 hours or until firm.

HUDDLE UP!

Typically known as a party punch, sangria can be changed up in any number of ways. The common elements are fruit and wine, but other ingredients such as fruit juice, carbonated soda, and other alcohol can be added.

ALCOHOL-BASED DRINKS

TWISTED 'RITAS

🏈 MAKES ABOUT 4 CUPS 🏈

In a 1-qt. mason jar, combine 1 cup of fresh lime juice, 1 cup of silver tequila, 1 cup of 7UP®, and 2 tablespoons of lime simple syrup*; add 1 sliced lime and fill with ice. Cover, shake, and strain into ice-filled glasses.

*For lime simple syrup, dissolve 1 cup of sugar in ½ cup each of water and fresh lime juice in a small saucepan; cool before using. Keep extra in the fridge for up to two weeks.

TAILGATE TRIVIA

Coolers are a MUST for tailgating! The first plastic cooler was introduced by Coleman in 1957.

ALCOHOL-BASED DRINKS

SIDELINE SLAMMERS

🏈 MAKES ABOUT 5¼ CUPS 🏈

In a 2-qt. pitcher or lidded jar, mix two 16.9-oz. bottles of Dr Pepper®, ¾ cup apple-flavored whiskey, and ¼ cup grenadine. Serve over ice.

HUDDLE UP!

To make these football-inspired drink glasses, cut white vinyl or label stickers to desired size and attach to dry glasses.

ALCOHOL-FREE DRINKS

"DAIQUIRI" DELIGHT

🏈 MAKES 4 SERVINGS 🏈

Combine 3 cups sliced strawberries and 6 tablespoons of apple juice in a blender; process until smooth and pour into a 1-qt. mason jar. Repeat with an additional 3 cups of berries and 6 tablespoons of juice. Stir in 6 oz. frozen limeade concentrate (thawed); cover and chill.

Divide chilled strawberry concentrate evenly among four 1-pt. mason jars. Add lime slices, ice, and ¼ to ½ cup of lemon-lime soda to each jar; stir. Garnish with sliced strawberries before serving, if desired.

GAME CHANGER!

To make these party-friendly mason jar sippers, you'll need rubber grommets with a hole at least ⅜" in diameter to hold a straw. Drill an off-center hole in a metal mason jar lid, 1⁄16" larger than the hole in the grommet (set lid on scrap wood to drill the hole). Fit the grommet into the hole. Fill the jar with your favorite beverage and attach the lid with the ring. Add your straw and sip!

TROPI-COOLER

🏈 **MAKES 4 SERVINGS** 🏈

Combine 1½ cup each of orange and pineapple juices, ¾ cup lemon juice, and ½ cup sugar; stir to dissolve. Pour mixture into a 1-qt. mason jar; cover and chill.

Divide citrus concentrate among four 1-pt. mason jars. Add ice and about ¼ cup plain or lemon-flavored soda water to each jar; stir. Garnish with sliced oranges or lemons before serving.

BEVERAGES

ALCOHOL-FREE DRINKS

MOCHA MIX

🏈 MAKES ABOUT 20 SERVINGS 🏈

Stir together 1 cup powdered coffee creamer, ¾ cup hot cocoa mix, ¾ cup instant coffee crystals, ¾ cup sugar, ½ teaspoon cinnamon, ¼ teaspoon ground nutmeg, and ¼ teaspoon salt. For each serving, put 2 tablespoons of mix into a mug and stir in 1 cup of boiling water. Store extra mix in an airtight container.

TAILGATE TRIVIA

The first paid professional football player was William "Pudge" Heffelfinger. In 1892, he was paid $500 to play for the Allegheny Athletic Association (against the Pittsburgh Athletic Club).

ALCOHOL-FREE DRINKS

CHAI LATTE

🏈 MAKES 2 SERVINGS 🏈

In a small saucepan, combine 2 cups of milk or almond milk, ¾ teaspoon cinnamon, ¼ teaspoon ground ginger, ⅛ teaspoon ground cloves, and 3 tablespoons maple syrup. Whisk to combine.

Heat over medium-high heat until the mixture is a nice warm drinking temperature, whisking occasionally.

Pour into mugs and top with whipped cream; sprinkle with cinnamon, ginger, and cloves if you'd like.

CAFÉ BAVARIAN MINT MIX

🏈 MAKES 8 SERVINGS 🏈

In a medium bowl, combine ¼ cup powdered creamer, ⅓ cup sugar, ¼ cup instant coffee granules, 2 tablespoons cocoa powder, and 2 crushed hard mint candies. Toss gently with hands until evenly incorporated. Pack mixture in a large zip-top plastic bag to store. To serve, mix 2 tablespoons coffee mixture with 1 to 1½ cups of hot water.

TAILGATE TRIVIA

The average tailgater spends about $500 per year on food for tailgating parties.

ALCOHOL-FREE DRINKS

ICED COFFEE

🏈 MAKES ABOUT 4 SERVINGS 🏈

Place ½ cup ground coffee in a 1-qt. mason jar and fill with water. Cover and let set at room temperature for 8 hours. Pour liquid through a coffee filter–lined strainer; repeat with a fresh filter. Discard solids and pour liquid into a clean 1-qt. jar. Add water to fill jar. Cover and chill.

To serve, fill a 1-pt. mason jar with ice and fill ⅔ full with coffee concentrate. Add a generous splash of half-and-half and 2 to 3 tablespoons of sweetened condensed milk; stir well and enjoy. Keep remaining concentrate chilled until needed.

INDEX